Words That Change Minds

Mastering the Language of Influence

Shelle Rose Charvet

For Judy,

Enjoy!

Shelle Rose Charvet

KENDALL/HUNT PUBLISHING COMPANY
4050 Westmark Drive   Dubuque, Iowa 52002

To my sons, Jason and Sammy,
who give me much joy and keep on teaching me,
to my Mum, Betty Rose,
for always being there,
in memory of my Dad, Frank Rose,
who taught me about intellectual rigour and humour,
and in memory of my Grandma, Katie Rose,
who kept asking me: "Who told you?"

Copyright© by Shelle Rose Charvet, Success Strategies

ISBN 0–7872–0803–5

Printed in the United States of America
10   9   8   7   6   5   4   3   2   1

Contents

Acknowledgments

I would like to thank all those people, too numerous to name who helped make this book possible, by developing the original ideas, by giving me valuable learning experiences, by sharing with me their expert opinions and feedback, and by allowing me to work and play with them, in personal and professional relationships.

Thank you to Richard Bandler, John Grinder, Leslie Cameron-Bandler, and Judith Delozier for their development of Neuro-linguistic Programming. A BIG thank you to Rodger Bailey for his creation of the Language and Behaviour Profile, which is the basis of this book and much of my work. And thanks to all the other developers, teachers and practitioners of NLP who have influenced my life and my work.

I would like particularly to thank Dr. Lorraine Bourque, from the Faculty of Education at the Université de Moncton in Moncton, New Brunswick for her insight, feedback and friendship. Many thanks to Dr. David Rosenbloom, Head of Pharmaceutical Services at Chedoke-McMaster Hospitals in Hamilton, Ontario for his ability to see and realize the potential of new ideas. Also Doug MacPherson, Assistant to the Director of District 6 of the United Steelworkers of America, for his feedback and support of my work. Thanks to Thelma Egerton of IBM Europe for being a great client and friend, as well as a great trainer, who has shared many laughs and a few tears with me over the years. And a big "Merci!" to Pierre Artigues (Señor), my former boss in Paris and always my friend, for teaching me more about intellectual rigour and helping me understand and adapt to living and working in France.

Thanks to Ainslie Smith for reading what I wrote on her island paradise in Georgian Bay and saying it was great. Thanks to Stever (alias Stephen Robbins) and Jay Arthur for their excellent ideas for a book title.

Most of all I wish to thank my family. My brothers, Michael Rose (my computer guru) and Professor Jonathan Rose, for learning and using the material and encouraging me to write the book. My sister-in-law, award-winning writer Barbara Wade Rose for her personal support and critical eye. My mother, Betty Rose, for helping out in many ways. My kids Jason and Sammy for being who they are. All my family for loving and encouraging me. I love you all.

Part One

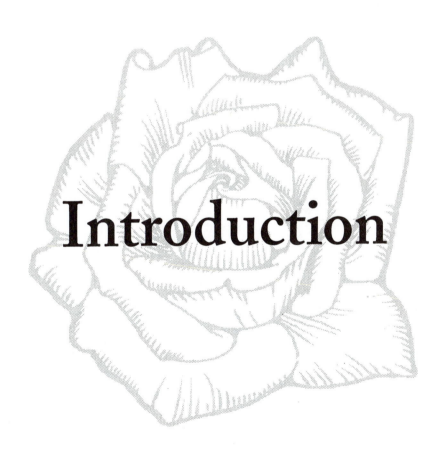

Introduction

Introduction

Words That Change Minds is built around a tool known as the Language and Behaviour Profile, or LAB Profile, created by Rodger Bailey. The LAB Profile is a development based on specific tools from *Neuro-linguistic Programming*.

Neuro-linguistic Programming

For those of you unfamiliar with Neuro-linguistic Programming, or NLP, here is my brief definition of what it is.[1]

Let's start with Programming. Each person, either through genetic make-up, environmental influences, or individual biochemistry, has managed to *program* her or himself to be excellent at a certain number of things, mediocre at different things and just awful in other areas. If we observe and listen carefully to how a person behaves and communicates *linguistically*, (in both verbal and nonverbal language), we can glean an understanding of how, *neurologically*, a person puts his or her experience together to be excellent, mediocre or awful at the things she or he does. Hence, this field is called Neuro-linguistic Programming.

The applications are enormous. It means if someone is highly skilled at something, and you are trained in certain NLP protocols, you can perform something called *modelling*. Modelling is finding out how it is possible for that person to do what she does. We search for the answers to questions such as: "What are the absolute essentials?" or "What is that person paying attention to or ignoring, sequentially and/or simultaneously, to be able to do it?" If you can discover the answers to these and other questions, then you can teach that skill or behaviour to other people and even learn it yourself.

The Language and Behaviour Profile is a model developed by Rodger Bailey, an avid student and developer in the field of NLP. He created the LAB Profile in the early 1980's. It is based on set of patterns from NLP called, at the time they were developed by Leslie Cameron-Bandler and others, the *Meta Programs*. These are the filters that we use to make up our *model of the world*.

---

1. For a very complete introduction to NLP, see **Introducing NLP.**, by Joseph O'Connor and John Seymour, (London: HarperCollins, 1993).

3

Creating Our Model of the World

Every person has a certain number of filters by which they let in certain parts of the real world. In Noam Chomsky's 1957 Ph.D thesis called **Transformational Grammar,** he said there are three processes by which people create the filters of their individual Model of the World, or their own personal reality:

Deletion

The first process is called **deletion.** We delete lots of information from the environment around us and internally. In his 1956 paper entitled **Seven plus or Minus Two.** George Miller, an American Psychologist, said that our conscious minds are only capable of handling seven plus or minus two bits of information at any one time, and that we delete the rest. That means on a good day you can handle nine and on a bad day maybe only five.

This explains why most telephone numbers are a maximum of seven digits. However, while I was living in Paris they changed the phone numbers to eight digits. What a mess. Everyone then had to decide whether to remember phone numbers by groups of two, or four, or to simply add the new Paris code, 4, onto the front of their old number. No one had an easy way of keeping eight digits in their head at once. Each person had to find their own way to break it down. That meant the people you were talking to would often give you phone numbers not necessarily in the way you had decided to group them. It created a great deal of confusion.

So seven plus or minus two bits of information is what we can be comfortably be aware of at one time. Using the process of deletion, we filter out lots of things without even being aware of it or consciously choosing to do so.

Distortion

The second process is called **distortion.** We distort things. Have you ever moved to a new place and gone into the living room before you moved your furniture in and pictured what it was going to look like furnished? Well, you were hallucinating. Your furniture was not *actually* in the room, was it? So you were distorting Reality.

Two examples of distortion are hallucination and creativity. They are both similar in that we change the external information to something else. That is what the process of distortion is all about.

Generalization

The last of the three processes we use to make up our model of the world is called **generalization.** It is the opposite of Cartesian Logic (where you can go from a general rule to specific examples but not the other way around).

Generalization is where you take a few examples and then create a general rule. This is how learning occurs. A small child learns to open one or two or possibly three doors and then she knows how to open all doors. The child develops a Generalization about how to open doors. That is, until she has to enter a high tech company and realizes that, to open the door, there is a magnetic card that has to be slid down a slot this way and not that way, and she has to relearn to deal with those exceptions.

Generalization is about how we make rules for ourselves, outside of our awareness. We have a number of experiences and we make a rule, which is part of how we create our own model of the world.

What is the link between these three processes, NLP and the LAB Profile? Richard Bandler and John Grinder, the co-originators of NLP, used deletion, distortion and generalization to create a map for discovering and influencing a person's perceptions and interpretations of their experiences.[2] Leslie Cameron-Bandler used them to build the Meta Programs, which she developed from her work in therapeutic settings. Rodger Bailey, a student of Leslie's, adapted and used her work in business settings. He created a tool which enables us to understand what people are communicating about their reality.

What is the Language and Behaviour Profile?

Language and Behaviour Patterns

When I first learned about Meta Programs, while working and studying in France, there were about 60 patterns. We had to talk to the people we were studying with and *guess* what their patterns were. I spent a year and a half trying to guess what everyone's Meta Programs were, and needless to say, I was not very good at it.

To make detecting and using these patterns simpler, Rodger Bailey had the genius to reduce the number of patterns from 60 to 14 and to develop a small set of specific questions. Regardless of what people answer to these well-designed questions, their unconscious personality patterns are revealed *in the structure* of the language they use. So we pay attention to *how* the person answers, instead of *what* they say. In this way, after asking a few simple questions, you can determine what will *trigger and maintain* someone's motivation.

---

2. Their map is called **The Meta Model.** Please see **The Structure of Magic 1** by Richard Bandler and John Grinder (Science and Behaviour Books, 1975).

Influencing Language

Secondly, he developed the *Influencing Language*. Once you know a person's patterns, you can then tailor your language so that it has *maximum impact* for that person. Using the right Influencing Language is extremely powerful because you are *speaking in someone's own personal style*.

To give you an analogy, imagine that someone who did not master your mother tongue very well was attempting to get some ideas across to you. Chances are that you would spend a lot of energy deciphering what they meant by translating it into terms that were more meaningful to you. When someone uses terms that you can *immediately* understand, no translation is necessary. They just go in.

You can choose precisely those **words that change minds**.

Using the LAB Profile

I have used the LAB Profile to create powerful presentations for large groups of people, redesign marketing and sales procedures to help companies to reach their major markets and to customize highly motivating messages for individuals in counselling. Now, wouldn't it be worthwhile learning a few questions that can do that for you?

As you become skilled at using the LAB profile, you will not always need to ask the questions. You will be able to simply listen, with your ears specifically tuned and eyes specifically focused and just pick up the patterns you are looking for. It is already all there, in how a person communicates.

And then there is the question of Reality.

Reality

I would like to make another point before we go on, just to avoid any confusion. From Noam Chomsky we know that people do not actually live in Reality. By deleting, distorting and generalizing, we inhabit our *perceptions* and *interpretations* of Reality. Because of this, I will NOT generally be dealing with Reality in this book, but rather the way we *perceive and interpret* it.

It is, however, important from time to time, to make reference to Reality. The occasional Reality Check as it were. Therefore, if I need to refer to Reality, I will warn you. Besides, do you know what Woody Allen said about Reality? He said something like: "Reality is the pits, but it's the only place you can get a good steak." So once in a while, one does need to refer to Reality.

What Happens When People Communicate?

Let's say a person has an experience. When that person talks about his experience, he only communicates a minute portion of the actual event. He has to edit out the vast majority of what was going on for him just to be able to communicate it in a reasonable time frame. It means that in order for you to tell someone about reading this book, you will need to eliminate most of what you experienced. You might say, "It was good," and nod your head, perhaps leaving out all the things this book made you think about, not mentioning whether you were physically comfortable at the time you were reading. Think of all those times when you did not grasp what someone was talking about because they left out the elements you needed to understand.

People accomplish this editing in a number of ways, primarily through *deleting, distorting and generalizing*. Knowing about these processes can make communication with other humans much easier. People transform their actual experience, their opinions, etc., in ways that correspond to their own particular Deletions, Distortions and Generalizations. With the LAB Profile, we now know *what it means* when they edit in certain ways. Rodger Bailey demonstrated that people who use the *same language patterns* in their speech have the *same behaviours*. In fact, from simple conversation we can listen to *how* a person communicates and pick up what will trigger and maintain his motivation, or what will make him change his mind. The Language and Behaviour Profile got its name from the connections between a person's language and how they behave.

The tools in this book will enable you to *predict and influence* behaviour. The LAB Profile is a set of tools that can be learned as a skill. You will have the opportunity to train your eyes and ears to perceive certain things that you may not have paid attention to before. You will also learn some ways of describing and working with behaviour patterns you had already noticed.

Because the LAB Profile is a set of skills, you will need to use it with a certain amount of care, paying attention to the shifts people make as they move from situation to situation. This is where the notion of Context comes in.

Context

The Context is the frame of reference a person puts around a situation. Since human beings are very rich and flexible by nature, they are able to behave differently at different times. Are we talking about you at work, in a couple relationship, with your kids, with your peers, when you are on holiday, or when you are buying a house? Simply because a person has a certain pattern or habit in a given place and time does not indicate that she will have that same pattern in another Context.

When I run seminars in this material, people ask me: "Am I always that way?" The answer is no. We move, we grow, and significant events in our lives can change how we function. Because our behaviour can vary in different situations, you will need to make sure when using the LAB Profile questions that you have clearly and specifically identified the Context. What is the frame of reference (or Context) around the situation for the person you are speaking with?

If used with integrity and care, The LAB Profile will enable you to dramatically improve all of your communication in many Contexts. But it is not magic, nor is it a miracle cure.

Miracle Cures

Many people are in the market for miracle cures; simple solutions to complex problems. While the LAB Profile can help you achieve remarkable outcomes in your life, it will take some effort and application on your part, and not just happen at the snap of your fingers. Remember when Nancy Reagan was in power with Ronald Reagan? She came up with an anti-drug program to stop kids taking drugs. It was called: **Just Say No**. I heard that a year later, deciding to build on success, she created a program to solve the problem of homelessness. It was called: **Just Get a House**. I understand that she was considering leaving the obscure life of retirement to publicize her latest idea; a program to combat unemployment. Can you guess what she called it?

People at work are facing more difficult challenges than ever before; pressure to change and perform in trying circumstances; to create harmony among groups of individuals to get them working towards the same goals, and do more with fewer resources. Hardly anyone can afford to rest on their laurels.

Even God has been feeling the heat.[3] Recently God was refused tenure at Hebrew University. Apparently, He[4] only had *one* publication; it had no references and there was even some doubt as to God's authorship of the book. The principal reason given was that, even if God *did* create the Earth, what has He done lately?

---

3. This information came directly from the Source, in Israel, to my brother at the University of Toronto.

4. My sons insist that God is a He.

It was also mentioned that the scientific community has been unable to replicate God's results.

The communication tools you will learn in this book will not only help you to think about what you do, but to act with greater precision in your work with others. These tools are important because they will enable you to prevent and avoid a lot of communication problems that you might not otherwise have foreseen. They will also help you move towards your goals. You will become aware of the results inside yourself and others will notice. These tools will help you progress in your growth, or totally change the things you want.

Think of what you'll achieve as you master **Words That Change Minds.**

Part Two

Motivation Traits

Motivation Traits

The first six categories in the LAB Profile will show you how different people trigger their motivation and what language you will need to use to capture their interest. Each category is dealt with in a separate chapter.

For each category of patterns you will learn the questions to ask, how to detect the patterns in ordinary conversation, what each person needs to get interested or excited about something, and conversely, what would turn them off.

There are no good or bad patterns to have. You can judge the appropriateness of each pattern only in the Context of the activity that needs to be done. For each pattern I have included ways to take advantage of the strengths and qualities inherent in each one.

While each category represents behaviour on a *continuum* from one pattern to another, **each pattern is described in its pure form. Behaviour predictions are only valid in the same Context in which the subject was profiled.**

After the behaviour description for each pattern you will find a section entitled **Influencing Language**. Listed here are examples of the kind of language which has the greatest impact. For each category the distribution of the patterns is shown. The figures are from the research that Rodger Bailey conducted, and are valid *only* for the work Context. They will give you an idea of how frequently you can expect to find certain patterns.

I will discuss the patterns in different situations, with lots of examples to provide insight and illustrate the fine points of using **Words That Change Minds**.

At the end of both the Motivation Traits and Working Traits section are **summary worksheets**, which can be used when profiling people. At the end of the book are complete profiling worksheets.

Waiting for Godot or Jumping at the Bit: Motivation Level

Does the person take the initiative or what for others?

This category in the Motivation Traits is about what will get you going and what will make you think. What is your LEVEL of activity? There are two patterns:

Proactive

Proactive people initiate. They tend to act with little or no consideration; to jump into situations without thinking or analyzing. They may upset some people because they can bulldoze ahead with what they want to do. They are good at going out and getting the job done. They do not wait for others to initiate.

Reactive

Reactive people wait for others to initiate or until the situation is right before they act. They may consider and analyze without acting. They want to fully understand and assess the situation before they will act. They believe in chance and luck. They will spend a lot of time waiting. Some people may get upset with them because they do not *get started*. They will wait for others to initiate and then respond. In the extreme, they operate with extra caution and study situations endlessly. They make good analysts.

DISTRIBUTION

(*in the work Context from Rodger Bailey*)

Proactive	Equally Proactive & Reactive	Reactive
15–20%	60–65%	15–20%

Since about 60 to 65% of the population in the work *Context* are Equally Proactive and Reactive, it is reasonable to assume that the person you are profiling is in the middle, unless they clearly demonstrate that they lean to one side or the other.

Pattern Recognition

Since there is no specific question to ask for this category, you can pay attention to the person's sentence structure and body language, as they will be giving you their pattern throughout your conversation.

Proactive—sentence structure

- short sentences: noun, active verb, tangible object
- speaks as if they are in control of their world
- crisp and clear sentence structure
- direct
- at the extreme, they "bulldoze"

Proactive—body language

- signs of impatience, speaking quickly, pencil tapping, lots of movement or inability to sit for long periods

Reactive—sentence structure

- incomplete sentences, subject or verb missing
- passive verbs or verbs transformed into nouns
- lots of infinitives
- speak as if the world controls them, things happen to them, believe in chance or luck
- long and convoluted sentences
- talks about thinking about, analyzing, understanding, or waiting, or the principle of the thing
- conditionals, would, could, might, may
- overly cautious, need to understand and analyze

Proactive—body language

- willingness to sit for long periods

Examples

Proactive: "I meet with my team every week."

Mainly Proactive: "I meet with my team if it seems like we need it."

Equally Proactive and Reactive: "I meet with my team to go over the current files. It is important to stay informed."

Mainly Reactive: "Even though you might wonder if it is necessary to meet with the team every week, I do it because it is important that they feel they are being listened to."

Reactive: "Even though everybody might wonder if it is really necessary to meet each week, it is important to consider the needs people have of being listened to."

Influencing Language

Just use these words and phrases to get people to jump into action. If you think about it, matching someone's way of being is very important when communicating.

Proactive	go for it; just do it; jump in; why wait; now; right away; get it done; you'll get to do; take the initiative; take charge; run away with it; right now; what are you waiting for; let's hurry
Reactive	let's think about it; now that you have analyzed it; you'll get to really understand; this will tell you why; consider this; this will clarify it for you; think about your response; you might consider; could; the time is ripe; good luck is coming your way

Since most people have some Proactive and Reactive, you can use both sets of Influencing Language; considering and doing.

Hiring

Proactive people are suitable for those positions which require taking the initiative, going out and getting it done. They would work well in outside sales, in independent businesses or the kind of work where having chutzpah[1] is an asset. If you are advertising for a highly Proactive person, ask the applicants to phone instead of sending in a résumé. (Reactive people will not phone.)

People who have a Reactive pattern in the work Context are well-suited to jobs that allow them to respond to requests. Representatives on customer service desks tend to be more Reactive. Many research and analytical jobs need someone who can spend a lot of time analyzing data.

Most people and most positions require a mixture of the two patterns. When hiring, you will need to examine what proportion of the work to be done consists of Reactive or Proactive activities to determine the kind of balance you need. It is appropriate to profile the others on the team to make sure you have an good balance.

There are some *key questions* to ask yourself regarding this category when profiling a position. To what degree will this person need to take the initiative? How much of the job consists of responding, analyzing or is dependent on the actions others? You might want to estimate the percentage of overall time in Proactive or Reactive activities.

Stepping on Toes: People Management

People who are very Proactive will be impatient with bureaucratic delays or internal politics, and may even go outside of their bounds, stepping on others' toes to get things done. They jump into activities and may go very far, very fast before you, or they, notice when they are on the wrong track. As the manager of Proactive employees, you will need to channel their energy in appropriate directions. If they do not have the opportunity to use their high level of energy, they will become frustrated or bored, and, as a result, may use their initiative in unproductive ways. You can motivate them by giving them a job to do and telling them to "Go for it." You may need to remind them to think before they jump.

Reactive people will generally not take initiatives and will feel stressed or anxious when asked to do so. At the extreme, they will want to consider, analyze and *be given* an understanding of situations almost to the exclusion of deciding or doing anything. In a team setting, Reactive people can contribute to the process by analyzing proposed solutions and slowing the process enough to consider ramifications and alternatives. You can motivate Reactive people by matching their pattern. "Now that you have had enough time to consider and think about this, I will need it on my desk by Monday at noon."

---

1. a Yiddish word, meaning having a lot of nerve

Fate and Destiny

Reactive people do not believe that they control their world. Chances are that they will be waiting for someone else to solve problems or make improvements for them. Do you remember Vladimir and Estragon in Samuel Becket's *Waiting for Godot?* They spent the entire play waiting for the mythical Godot to appear and solve all their problems.

Since most people at work are somewhere in the middle, they will need to think and do, respond and initiate. The best kinds of work for these people are tasks and responsibilities that allow enough of each. To motivate these people you would use both sets of influencing language. For example, "I would like you to think through what needs to be done and just go do it."

Sales and Marketing

Proactive people tend to buy when they get to do something right away. One day over coffee, I suggested doing a LAB Profile to help a prospective client decide on a career change. I told her that the profile would immediately show her what kinds of activities would trigger and maintain her motivation. She enthusiastically agreed and wanted to do it right then. As we were walking back to my office she said: "Can we run?" She has an off-the-scale Proactive pattern in that Context.

Reactive people will buy when the product or service allows them to gain understanding. They will often be waiting for something to happen before they will decide. I went to see the CEO of a company that sells mutual funds, to talk about sales training for his sales representatives. At our *third* meeting, he told me that the company was completing a merger and he was "waiting for the situation to be clarified." As a highly Proactive person, the voice in my head exploded and said, "What do you want, a message from God? *Who* is going to clarify the situation?" I managed to control the impulse and asked: "Oh, and when is this likely to happen?" I used that phrase to match his belief that things happen *to* him.

Reactive people will be more likely to buy if you suggest that this is what they have been waiting for, or "Haven't you waited long enough to get what you really want?" Or "Once you have this, you'll understand why. . . . "

You will occasionally notice marketing campaigns that call to Proactive or Reactive people. They may also reveal aspects of the company's corporate culture. In 1993, a large Canadian bank had a slogan: "Get us working for you." My interpretation was that I, as a potential customer, was going to have to wake them up and make them do something for me. But perhaps that way of looking at it is a result of my propensity for being Proactive.

You may have noticed NIKE's slogan: "Just do it." A call to action for the Proactive sorts.

Golden Handshakes

During the early to mid 1990's, large corporations and subsequently governments decided they needed to shed large numbers of workers. In order to accomplish these large-scale layoffs, many organizations used the *Golden Handshake* approach, offering an attractive package to those who would take the money and leave.

Can you guess who took the money and jumped ship? Have you noticed that this period also coincided with the largest ever increase in home-based businesses?

Proactive people jump at the Golden Handshake as a chance to go out and set up their own operations. Organizations lost many of their most dynamic people. One friend told me that her boss said: "Oh, but we didn't want *you* to leave!" Too late buddy.

My suggestion to organizations is to plan any necessary lay offs by first deciding *which roles to keep*. (Easier said than done, I know.) The roles will probably call for a mixture of Proactive and Reactive, as well as many of the other patterns described in this book. I then suggest that particular people be offered the buy-out package; those who do not fit the desired profiles. Also, I believe it is important to offer counselling to those who will be leaving, to help them make decisions and set up their next steps.

SUMMARY

LEVEL

Proactive: Acts with little or no consideration. Motivated by doing.
Reactive: Motivated to wait, analyze, consider and react.

Distribution at Work: Proactive 15–20%
                           Equally 60–65%
                           Reactive 15–20%

INFLUENCING LANGUAGE

Proactive: do it; jump in; get it done; don't wait
Reactive: understand; think about; wait; analyze; consider; wait; might; could; would

Pushing Those Hot Buttons: Criteria

> What are the words that will incite a physical and emotional response?

I asked Simone: "What do you want in your work?" She replied: "*A challenge, something that allows me to utilize my present skills and develop new ones, good remuneration and working with people.*"

Those are the things that are important to Simone in her work. Now what does this mean? Simone has given me her *Criteria* for work.

Criteria is the term we use to describe a person's way of making distinctions about what is good, bad, awful, wrong, right, etc. They are personal labels. Many of these words are labels for our values.

A person's Criteria are those words which *incite a physical and emotional reaction*; **HOT BUTTONS**. The words themselves are associated, or stuck in our memory, to a series of emotionally similar events that we have experienced through our lives. So when a person hears one of her Criteria, *the word itself* will trigger the emotional response attached to it.

We each have our own definition for each Criterion. A single Criterion is composed of many elements, conscious and unconscious. You may never need to know a person's definition of her Criteria in those situations where you simply want to find out *how* she describes something she is excited about in a given Context.

Here's an illustration of *negative hot buttons*. In any family, each of you know the others' negative hot buttons. For example, the other members of your family know that if they say a particular word or phrase, you will explode. In my family, one son need only say to the other: "Nope, you're wrong!" to create an explosion of frustration. An emotional and physical reaction.

Many people took interpersonal communication courses in the 1970's and 80's and sometimes even today, where they learned Active Listening, based on Carl Rogers' work. Active Listening consists of paraphrasing what the other person said, *in your own words*, in order to show him what you understood. We can now appreciate that if Simone says that she wants "a challenge" and I play back to her, "so you want something challenging," it does not *create* the same experience for her. When I paraphrase into my own words what you say, it has more to do with my reality than your reality, and nothing whatever to do with Reality with a capital R. To solve this problem, we now teach participants in communication courses, that to show someone you have understood them, you will need to play back *their* key words, their Criteria.

Other questions to elicit Criteria:

What do you want in . . . (a job, a home, a spouse, etc.)?

What's important to you?

What counts?

What *has* to be there?

What would you like to have, be or do?

What to Do With Criteria

Making Decisions: A Hierarchy of Criteria

Knowing how to uncover and work with Criteria can give you an infallible means of deciding what is more important and what is less important in a given Context. You can do this for yourself and with other people. I'll demonstrate with Simone. This technique is called making a **Hierarchy of Criteria.**

SRC: Simone, you had a number of things that were impor-
          tant for you at work. Let's list them.

Simone: A challenge, something that allows me to utilize my
          present skills and develop new ones, good remunera-
          tion and working with people.

We have four Criteria here and we do not yet know which are essential, optional, or which are the most important for Simone. I, as the listener may think one is more important than another for her, but that would be hallucinating.

SRC: Simone, imagine for a moment that I have a couple of
          jobs that might fit your needs. In this hand over here
          (holding out my left hand, palm up), you will get a job
          with a *challenge.* And in this hand, (holding out my
          right hand, palm up; hands wide apart), this job allows

you to *utilize your present skills and develop new ones.* Which one attracts you?

Simone:	A challenge.

If you observe carefully, (which is *a challenge* to illustrate in a book) you can often see the choice being made before the person says anything. It is important to keep your hands wide apart so the person will perceive two *separate* choices. I do not know exactly how Simone is processing this choice, but by putting each option in a different hand, I am creating something more real or tangible for her in each hand.

How would I write down her choice if I were taking notes? An easy and quick way is to draw an arrow from *challenge* down to *allows me . . .* to indicate that challenge is "over" allows me.

SRC:	In my right hand is a job that will offer you *a challenge.* In my left is one that has *good remuneration.* If you **had** to choose, which one would you want?
Simone:	Hmmm. A challenge.
SRC:	So challenge is the most important so far. OK, in my left hand is a job with a challenge and in my right hand is a job where you'll be working with people. Which one do you want?
Simone:	Still a challenge.

We now know that *a challenge* is the most important of these Criteria for Simone, in the Context of work. To complete the Hierarchy we will need to compare each of the other options to each other as we just did.

SRC:	Simone, in this hand is a job which allows you to *utilize your present skills and develop new ones,* and over here is one with *good remuneration.* Which one would you take?
S:	Good remuneration.
SRC:	Over here *good remuneration* and in this hand *working with people?*
S:	Good remuneration.
SRC:	And lastly, *working with people* in this hand, and *allows you to utilize your present skills and develop new ones* in this hand?
S:	Working with people.

Now we have Simone's Criteria in order of importance to her:

1. A challenge
2. Good remuneration

3. Working with people
4. Allows me to utilize my present skills and develop new ones

For those of you who help people make decisions, as in sales, this is a very useful process to take your customers through. It can also be used when coaching employees or counselling clients. I also use it for career counselling, where I would need to get the client to define what would constitute each Criterion.

The easiest way to get someone to define their Criteria is to ask: "Can you give me an example of something that was *a challenge?*" This works well because often people cannot give a straight definition of terms for something that is directly attached to a series of memories and emotions.

The Hierarchy of Criteria is also used to make some decision-making processes much shorter. This is a way of helping people get their mind, soul and body to decide. When you create a tangible, forced choice situation, people will feel magnetically attracted to one option or the other.

Can't Make Up Your Mind?

Sometimes a person will have difficulty choosing between the two alternatives in your hands and you can confirm this by observing the vacillation in their body as they try to choose. What does this mean, and what do you do about it? There are five situations where this occurs that I have identified to date:

1. The person did not accept the idea that they *have* to choose between two things they want.
2. One Criterion is a component of the other one.
3. The person has two labels for the same set of experiences.
4. One Criterion causes the other to occur.
5. The person has a conflict between two values or Criteria.

As in the first case, if the person refuses to choose, you will need find a way to get them to play along. You can ask them to imagine that *if they had to choose*, knowing that in real life, they can actually have both, but if they *had* to choose, which one would attract them?

Sometimes they cannot choose because one Criterion is a component of the other. In other words, one Criterion is *contained within* another Criterion. You can test for this by asking "Is *allows you to utilize your present skils and develop new ones* part of *a challenge* for you? Or the other way around?" In that case you can include the component within the larger Criterion and only use the larger one. "So when we're talking about *a challenge*, we know it includes *allows you to utilize your present skills and develop new ones."*

Another possibility is that the person has two labels for the same set of experiences. If it means the same thing, he would have difficulty choosing between 'it' and 'itself'. For example let's say a person cannot choose between *interesting* and *a challenge*. To test for this, you can simply ask: "Are *interesting* and *a challenge* really the same thing for you?" If the persons says: "Yes, it is always interesting when there's a challenge," you know that they are closely linked (in his mind anyway). In this case you might want to use both labels to stay in rapport with that person.

The fourth situation is when one Criterion *causes* the other other to occur in a cause-effect relationship. You can check this by asking: "Does having *a challenge* make you *utilize your present skills and develop new ones?"*

The fifth possibility for an unclear choice between two options presented in this manner is that the person has a conflict between two values or Criteria. They will waver back and forth and "yes, but" to themselves or out loud. You can predict, in this case, that the person will have difficulty making certain decisions in this Context and will feel in a "stuck" state. Remember Tevye in Fiddler on the Roof, "On one hand . . . on the other hand . . . ?"

Difficult to Satisfy?

What does it mean when you ask someone "What do you want?" or "What's important?" and the person lists off 15 or 20 things? It means that this person is difficult to satisfy. If she has 15 or 20 Criteria and has no idea which ones are more important than the others, she will have a difficult time making decisions or even being able to find exactly what she wants. Can you imagine a woman finding the man of her dreams with 15 Criteria?

What is a decision? Often making a decision consists of choosing between two or more alternatives. One of the biggest favours you can do for a person who has many undifferentiated Criteria, is to take him through a Hierarchy of Criteria, and then have him create a bottom line cut-off on what absolutely must be there and what is optional.

Uses for Criteria

If you are considering buying a product for example, what *must* it have? If you are considering getting married, what are the most important things for you in the person and the relationship? Remember that when you change Context your Criteria may change. Many people do not want the same thing in a house that they want in a spouse.

In the process of goal-setting, you need to list the Criteria for success and understand which are more important. We know that those people who have clearly defined Criteria for their goals are more likely to achieve them quickly. By defining your Criteria, you will have made them real and tangible to yourself.

One of the gentlemen I trained in this technique is a Real Estate broker. When he hires people he uses the Hierarchy of Criteria to find out whether the candidates have the priorities about work that he would like them to have. He asks them "What is important for you in your work?" He then casually asks: "If you *had* to choose between a job where you got to be a *team player* (putting out his left hand) and one where you could be *your own boss* (putting out his other hand), which one would you pick?"

If you are going to start a project with someone or select members of a team or task force, you might want to check out what is important to each prospective member. Do they have the values you are looking for? You can ask them these questions: What do you want from this project? What do you want in a company? What do you want in a team? What's more important to you? This, (holding it one hand), or this? You will find that it is very easy to build this into ordinary conversation.

Influencing with Criteria: A Powerful Sales and Marketing Tool

The gathering of Criteria is a necessary prerequisite for sales and any kind of influencing or persuading process. Unskilled sales people just *pitch their product* (usually using their own Criteria) without much regard to what their prospective customer actually wants. "Lady, this car has everything you want; good mileage, great handling and flashy decals on the side!" This is what I call the 'shot in the dark' approach. Who knows? They might actually hit something.

Many market researchers investigate people's Criteria so that the exact phrasing of an advertising campaign can match what is most important to the groups they wish to influence.

If you want to get and keep someone's interest you will need to link what you are proposing with their Criteria. I even use this when public speaking by doing a question and answer session before I begin the body of my talk. I will often ask an audience "What's important to you when you communicate?" Or "What would you want to do if you knew how to predict and influence behaviour?" If someone tells me they want to "know how to present their proposals in a negotiation so that they will be accepted," then I make sure to link those Criteria with the points I am making.

Many people underestimate the power of matching someone's Criteria. Once, as a demonstration with a group, I told a woman about a job opportunity, using all her highly held Criteria. I did not tell her what the job *was*, I simply used her Criteria: "You'll really be needed, people will appreciate what you do for them, you'll be in charge of how you work and the hours are regular." She said she would take the job, without even finding out what it was. I know someone who moved from New England to California for a career opportunity that *matched* his Criteria, only to find that the work and the company did not at all meet his expectations. You will need to be careful to deliver what you promise when you use someone's Criteria to persuade them. Otherwise their disappointment and anger will likely be directed at you. Just ask the leaders of all the governments thrown out of office by disenchanted voters.

Remember, to influence with Criteria, you will need to state them *exactly* as the other person expressed them. They are the triggers to bringing up emotions.

SUMMARY

CRITERIA

A person's labels for things are important to them in a given Context. They are *hot buttons* because they are attached to emotions and memories.

INFLUENCING LANGUAGE

Use the person's Criteria to attract and maintain their interest. When a person hears his own Criteria, he will immediately feel the emotions attached to those words.

The Carrot or the Stick:
Motivation Direction

> What will trigger a person into action? What *direction* do they move in? Do they move *towards* an objective, or *away from* problems to be solved or prevented?

When you master this category, you will be able to prevent and avoid many problems as well as know how to reach your goals more effectively.

There are two patterns in this category which describe the *Direction* a person is moving, in a given Context. They are either moving **toward** a goal, or **away from** problems. Each pattern is first described in its pure form.

Toward

Toward people stay focused on their goal. They think in terms of goals to be achieved. They are motivated to have, get, achieve, attain, etc. Because of their concentration on goals to be accomplished, they tend to be good at managing priorities. Moreover, they are energized by their goals.

People with a strong Toward pattern often have trouble either recognizing what should be avoided, or in identifying problems. At the extreme, they are perceived as naive by others because they do not take potential obstacles into account.

Away From

Away From people notice what should be avoided, gotten rid of and otherwise not happen. Their motivation is triggered when there is a problem to be solved or when there is something to move away from. They are energized by threats. A salesperson told me: "If I don't get out there and sell, I won't be able to pay my bills at the end of the month." Deadlines, for example, get this people into action. People with an Away From pattern in a given Context are good at trouble-shooting, solving problems, and at pinpointing possible obstacles during planning because they automatically pick up on what is wrong.

They may have trouble maintaining focus on their goals because they are easily distracted and are compelled to respond to negative situations. This is the kind of person who will drop everything to fix something. At the extreme they forget what the priorities are and only concentrate on treating crises. If this person is at the top of a department or an organization, the *entire organization will be run by crisis management.* Away From people have some difficulty managing priorities because whatever is wrong will attract most of their attention. People who have a strong Away From orientation in a given Context are often perceived as jaded or cynical, particularly by Toward people.

DISTRIBUTION

(*in the work Context, from Rodger Bailey*)

	Equally	
Toward	**Toward & Away From**	**Away From**
40%	20%	40%

Most people will be mainly Toward or mainly Away From on this continuum, in a given Context.

Pattern Recognition

QUESTIONS:

- **Why is having that** (their Criteria) **important?**

  or
- **What will having that** (Their Criteria) **do for you?**

Toward—sentence structure

- talks about what they gain, achieve, get, have etc.
- inclusion
- what they want, goals

Toward—body language

Pointing towards something, head nodding, gestures of inclusion

Away from—sentence structure

- will mention situations to be avoided, gotten rid of
- exclusion of unwanted situations, things
- problems

Away from—body language
Gestures of exclusion, shaking head, arms indicating that something is to be avoided, gotten rid of

Note: Listen to what the person says after the word **because**. It will either be a Toward or an Away From statement.

Examples

Toward: "I would get personal satisfaction and a promotion."

Mainly Toward: "I would get a promotion, personal satisfaction, make more money and not have to go on the road."

Equally Toward and Away From:
"I would get personal satisfaction and not have to go on the road."

Mainly Away From: "I would not have all this routine work, or be away from my family often; plus I would get a promotion."

Away From: "I would get away from this boring work, all the deadlines, and my boss who keeps looking over my shoulder."

You will need to ask the questions in a series or laddering approach, as follows:

SRC: Adam, can you give me your Criteria for a job?
A: Effective, more proficient, fun and taken seriously.
SRC: All right, Adam, *why is having that important?*
A: To *help people.*
SRC: To help people. And why is that important?
A: Because I *get satisfaction* from helping people.
SRC: So why is satisfaction important?
A: Well, *that's what I want* from a job.

Here's a different example:

SRC: Joanne, what do you want in a job?
J: I like to know what I have to do, and to be evaluated based on my own performance.
SRC: Why is that important?
J: It *gives me a sense of calm.*
SRC: And what's important about that?
J: If *I'm not calm with myself, I can't be calm with my kids.*
SRC: And why is that important?
J: *It keeps me from hitting my kids.*

Joanne wanted to have her Criteria met in order to prevent a certain outcome, while Adam was motivated to attain his Criteria in order to achieve an outcome.

The reason we ask the Motivation Direction questions several times is to get a more accurate sense of where the person puts their energy; *towards goals* or *away from* problems. In my experience, when we ask the question only once, we usually get a one-line Toward answer, regardless of the person's actual pattern. I believe that is because many of us have subscribed to the "Power of Positive Thinking" and so, devalue the importance of recognizing problems.

There was an elderly gentleman who resided at a hotel. Every evening he shuffled gingerly to the front desk to get his keys and over to the elevator to go up to his room. One day he got his keys and went up the elevator as usual, only to immediately return to the front desk. He addressed the clerk: "Young lady, I have a problem." The bright young employee had been trained in customer service and the power of positive thinking, so she replied: "We don't have problems here sir, we have challenges!" The gentleman snorted and said: "Harumph! I don't know if it's a problem or a challenge, but there is a woman in my room."

So we ask the questions about three times to find out what is behind, or what is triggering the person into action in that Context.

Alternate Questions:

What's the point?

Why bother?

What's important about X?

What's in that for you?

So, Why Did You Leave Your Last Job?

Changes in Context

Why did you leave your last job? Because you couldn't stand it any more? Or because there was something better on the horizon? Why did you leave your last spouse? Because you were unhappy, or because there was someone else on the horizon? Why did you take your last vacation? Was it because you wanted a break from the grind or because you were interested in doing something in particular?

You may have a Toward pattern in one Context and an Away From pattern in another Context.

Can your Direction change over time? Yes it can. A single significant event may change your pattern. Let's say someone has a Toward pattern and has all kinds of habits that probably are not good for his health. Then he has a heart attack and what happens? Because the heart attack was a very nasty, yet compelling experience, he may change Direction, and begin moving *away from* health problems. He might change his behaviour, quitting smoking, doing more exercise, changing his diet, etc., because he *does not want* to have another heart attack. Some addiction treatment programs work on that basis.

Sometimes people do not make changes in their lives because they have not yet hit rock bottom. A helpful question might be: "Do you *feel bad enough now* to make some changes or would you rather wait until you feel *even worse?*"

Influencing Language

Using the Influencing Language appropriately, will get you a person's complete attention. That will prevent you from having to repeat things several times. The rapport that you establish will be deeper because you have matched how the person thinks and you will not have to spend a lot of time in order to get on the same wavelength. Because you have established rapport, you can avoid a lot of misunderstandings.

Here are some typical expressions to use:

Toward
- attain; obtain; have; get; include; achieve; enable you to; benefits; advantages; here's what you would accomplish

Away From
- won't have to; solve; prevent; avoid; fix; prevent; not have to deal with; get rid of; it's not perfect; let's find out what's wrong; there'll be no problems

What Would Make You Set and Attain Goals?

For many years people have been teaching and learning about the importance of setting goals. It has been proven many times, that if you do not have goals, chances are you will not be able to find what you truly want. Was that last sentence a Towards statement or an Away From statement? It was Away From. You don't get anywhere if you don't have goals.

When we are discussing a person's Motivation Direction, we are talking about what will **trigger** her into doing something, such as setting goals. Why do *I personally* set goals in my business? Because if I didn't I would be totally disorganized. I do set goals, and I have an **Away** From pattern at work. For me, this means that I can get distracted by whatever squeaks the loudest. In order to stay focused on what I am to achieve (and particularly so as *not* to become disorganized), about every 2 weeks I ask myself: "What business am I in?" This helps me recenter on what I really need to be doing. Another useful question for Away From people to ask themselves is: "How does this activity fit in with what I want to accomplish?"

Toward people need to ask themselves: Are my plans going to work? What else do I need to predict? What haven't I thought of yet that may go wrong? They may need the services of a devil's advocate in order to make sure they are being realistic.

There is a need for a balance in many situations. A good balance of Toward and Away From on a team will help ensure that goals are set, well-laid contingency plans are made, and focus is kept on priorities.

Is It Fear of Success or Motivation Direction?

Here's another consideration regarding Away From people and goal achievement. Let me give you an example. This happened to a therapist I know. He had a client who came to see him and said: "I'm very upset. My life is really going down the tubes. I've been a millionaire 4 times." At first glance you might say, "You've been a millionaire 4 times. So what's the problem?" Let's think about it. If he has been a millionaire 4 times, that means he lost it 3 times. So let's look at what happened.

The therapist asked him some questions and found out that he had an extreme Away From pattern about work. He was motivated *to move away from poverty*. Let's put this on a graph to understand his pattern. On the vertical axis, we have his amount of motivation, or how motivated he is, from not very motivated at the bottom to very motivated at the top. Let's put revenue on the horizontal axis, zero revenue to 1 million dollars. If he is highly motivated away from poverty, at zero revenue, how motivated is he? Very motivated. As he earns money, what happens? His interest level declines as his revenue increases. Once poverty was not an issue, he would not finish work on contracts, or he would forget to submit quotes to potential clients, or procrastinate and not follow up. When the big contract would come that could push him over the million dollar point, he says "Ahh, I'll do it when I get around to it." Whereas when he is threatened by poverty (whatever that means to him), he is highly motivated to do whatever it takes to generate revenue.

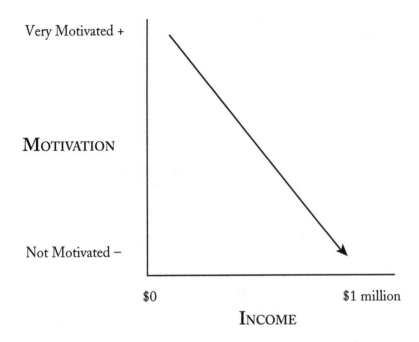

Very Motivated +

MOTIVATION

Not Motivated −

$0 $1 million

INCOME

Although this is an extreme example, it explains why highly Away From people need to recenter on what they are trying to achieve at regular intervals.

Positive or Negative Thinking?

When first acquainted with these patterns, many people judge people with a Toward pattern as positive, while the Away From pattern is seen as negative. This judgement comes from interpretations of the *Power of Positive Thinking*. Remember that these patterns are simply triggers which will catapult someone into action.

Mother Teresa was quoted as saying that she started her work when "I discovered there was a Hitler in my heart." Her Motivation Direction is Away From. Many lobby groups, such as Greenpeace, the National Action Committee for the Status of Women (NAC), the anti-nuclear movement, Amnesty International, etc., are essentially motivated to move away from certain practices that they do not agree with. You can therefore predict that these groups will notice what is insufficient or wrong with government legislation to protect the environment, rape shield laws, nuclear safety regulations, welfare reform, etc. Many journalists also have this pattern.

Here is a statement by **Nelson Mandela**, on **May 24, 1994**, the day he became President of South Africa:

> *"My government's commitment to create a people-centred society of liberty binds us to the pursuit of the goals of*

(at first glance this sounds pretty Toward, doesn't it?)

> *freedom from hunger, freedom from deprivation, freedom from ignorance, freedom from suppression and freedom from fear."*

If a person answers "freedom" in response to *Why is that important?*, do not assume that it is either Toward or Away From. Probe to find out if it is freedom *to* or freedom *from*.

Conflicts of Language in Labour Relations

In the Context of labour relations and negotiations, conflict arises *not only* because of the often contrary vested interests of labour and management. Conflict also arises because of the *cultural differences* between the two groups. If I can make a generalization for a moment, let's take top management as a culture. Is top management mainly Toward or Away From? Goals, business plans, objectives, etc., are Toward activities. What is the primary reason for the existence of a union? To make another generalization, unions often exist to *protect* their members *from disasters*; poor pay, bad working conditions, lay offs, etc.

Frequently, management and labour do not speak the same language. Management tends to negotiate in terms of moving toward its objectives while labour attempts to prevent certain things from occurring.

In 1995 the Canadian rail strike/lockout between Canadian National Railway (CN) and Canadian Pacific Railway (CP) on the one hand, and the Canadian Auto Workers (CAW) and the Brotherhood of Maintenance of Way Employees (BMWE) on the other gave clear examples of these patterns at work. The principal issue was over employment security, a hard won benefit that the unions were determined to *prevent* the railways from changing, particularly in the face of possible privatization of CN and massive layoffs. The railways were equally determined to modify the contract in order to *increase* their competitiveness with American railways and the trucking industry. In this example, each side was moving in a different Direction and, as is the case in labour disputes which escalate, were operating out of different Criteria.

If labour and management could each learn to understand the patterns of the other side, and learn how to speak in their language, they would improve their chances of reaching agreement with less strife.[2] Of course, in Reality, not all unions have an Away From motivation, nor do all employers have a Toward pattern.

Professions Have Cultures

Some professions are inherently Toward or Away From. For example, medicine as it is usually practised in the West, is highly Away From. As a culture, (as distinct from individual patterns) medical practitioners tend to focus on what is wrong with their patients. They move *away from sickness and dying*. I recently completed profiling all the pharmacists in a hospital and found that, out of 17 Pharmacists, 14 were mainly or highly Away From. The other three were only slightly on the Toward side of the equation. As a culture, the medical professions are so Away From, that when the idea occurred to them that holistic health might be something worth considering, they called it *Preventative Medicine*.

The Away From orientation is appropriate for treating and curing (getting rid of) disease. Can you imagine rushing in to your doctor about a medical emergency, and when you see her, she ignores your symptoms only to ask you about your health goals?

On the other hand, a number of people who are medical practitioners, work outside the traditional medical structures. I am willing to bet that many herbologists, iridologists and others, have a Toward pattern about their work and do not feel comfortable with people who primarily seek out and destroy disease.

As you read about the different patterns, you may find that you can deduce the cultural patterns of different professions.

Hiring

If you are going to hire someone, it would be useful to know whether the day-to-day activities of the job consist mainly of trouble-shooting and problem-solving or rather concentrating on the attainment of objectives. Although most organizations are now, at the very least, paying lip service to performance appraisals based on employee objectives, you will need to examine the day-to-day realities of the position more closely.

---

2. For much more complete information on how to negotiate, please see Fischer and Ury's **Getting to Yes**, Ury's **Getting Beyond No**, and Fischer's **Beyond Machiavelli**.

I assisted a design and manufacturing firm in hiring a plant manager. To do this I needed a list of responsibilities and tasks that this person would perform. The tasks included monitoring production reports and investigating causes of errors in production, shipping and data entry; ensuring that shipments are properly done; quality control; government compliance; negotiating with suppliers and facility maintenance. With the possible exception of negotiating with suppliers, most of the activities needed to meet these responsibilities required looking for, preventing and solving problems. A Toward Plant Manager would have missed many of the potential errors and omissions while charging ahead to meet production targets. (I have noticed that many people who have an Away From pattern call targets "*deadlines*.") I also profiled the senior management to ensure there would be a balance in the team, and that someone would be looking out to make sure objectives were met.

If you want to hire someone who is motivated to perform the job at hand, it is important to determine whether the job is goal-oriented or is mainly trouble-shooting. Do you need someone who is excited about working toward goals, or someone who delights in solving crises?

I will deal with how to write career advertisements to *only attract the 'right' candidates* in the Applications section of the book.

People Management and Task Assignment: The Carrot or the Stick

Since most managers already have a team of existing employees, they would be well advised to discover what their strengths are and to capitalize on those strengths, instead of suffering from the weaknesses.

To get and keep Toward employees motivated, they will need tasks that allow them to attain goals. You can tell them the benefits of doing a certain task, such as *improving* efficiency, *increasing* departmental revenue or *receiving a bonus*. In meetings they will want to stay focused on the objective and will have little patience for discussions about what might or is going wrong. They will consider such talk as *off topic*. You will need to explain to them the benefits of discussing potential problems and make sure you do that in Toward terms: "If we discuss and plan for potential problems now we'll reach the objective that much sooner," is more appropriate than: "If we don't look at problems now, we'll be unprepared later."

Toward employees, particularly when they also have a Proactive pattern, if left to charge on to their goals, may get some nasty surprises later due to inattention to potential hurdles.

Away From employees will steer meetings into discussions of obstacles and what is wrong with proposals. To help them be most productive in

meetings, explain to them (in Away From terms) why keeping the goal in mind will *prevent the group from losing focus*, which could be a major *waste of resources* and allot them time for *disaster prevention*. For tasks, give them problems to solve and things to fix. Impending disaster will energize them. "If this isn't out on time, they'll have our heads." The worst thing that you, as a manager, could do to an Away From employee is to take away all their problems. "Nothing's wrong, I'm worried." You, as a manager, may also not want to cope with the results of giving a Toward task to an Away From employee.

I suggest that you do not ask a Toward employee to proofread a document. They will not pick out the errors. If you notice mistakes in text as if they jumped out of the page, then you have an Away From pattern in the Context of reading. I gave the first draft of this book to a friend to read over, having forgotten about her Toward pattern. Apart from adding a couple of commas, she said: "It's just great," and went on to tell me all the things she liked about it.

The Cure to Writers' Block

When you write letters, reports, articles or books, do you ever suffer from Writer's Block? If this happens regularly, then you probably have an Away From pattern in this Context. It is much easier, and more motivating, for Away From people to correct mistakes than it is for them to remain focused on the goal of their text.

My philosophy is to work from my strengths, as opposed to suffering from my weaknesses. So, knowing about my Away From pattern, I decided to write this book by doing what I do best: Fixing what's there. To do this, I had my audio tape series on the same topic, transcribed and put onto diskette. Then I structured the book, and imported sections of the transcript. Lastly I did the fun part. I corrected the text, looking for errors and omissions, needed updates and new examples.

I told my sister-in-law who is a writer, that I was able to produce about 22 pages of text per day. She found this to be incredible until I explained that: "I *wasn't writing* 22 pages, I *was correcting* 22 pages and adding in what was missing."

My advice to those of you who suffer from Writer's Block is to get *anything* down on paper (or up on the screen), even if you have to ask someone else to draft a letter, for example. Then fix it. It will be much less tedious and you won't waste a lot of time wondering what to say.

Of course this trick would not help you if you *really* had nothing to say.

A very toward dog!

Sales and Marketing

Just out of curiosity, I phoned up the local Automobile Association, and asked: "Why do people buy your service?" They told me that 90% of their members join the club to avoid problems such as breaking down and having to pay a fortune for a tow. In the Context of travel by car, the vast majority of their members therefore have an Away From pattern.

I recently had the opportunity to work with this Association. To explain what I meant by Toward and Away From, I took the management down to the front desk to eavesdrop on what customers were saying. Person after person said that they *didn't want to have to deal with* breakdown problems, expensive alternatives, etc. As a result we redesigned their marketing, sales and customer service processes to use mainly Away From language. "Your one-stop worry-free travel agency," "You won't have to deal with . . . ," "You needn't worry about . . . ," "No fee travellers cheques," "This will save you time," etc.

Insurance is another Away From product. Most customers buy to avoid problems for themselves or their families. Investments, on the other hand are inherently Toward. Imagine the difficulty insurance sales people must have had when insurance companies also began offering investment opportunities. They would have had to get their insurance customers into Toward thinking. Often they merely continued the pattern; pointing out the financial disasters inherent in not investing wisely.

As a salesperson or marketing director, there are several options you could take when planning your sales approach or marketing campaign. You can examine your product or service to discover if it is Toward or Away From by its very nature and design your process to attract more of the appropriate market segment. Alternatively, especially if your product or service could be both, you could design your strategy to be able to adapt to either, based on your individual customer's triggers. Another option is simply to find out who is already buying your product or service regardless of the characteristics of the product, and gear everything to increase your market share within that group. Or, if you have already saturated that group, you may judge it appropriate to go after the other pattern by using the correct Influencing Language.

Many books on sales will tell you that a person will buy either to *gain a benefit* or to *avoid a problem*. Once you have asked the question *Why is that important?*, to determine a Toward or Away From motivation, you can use the appropriate Influencing Language. If you want to sell a house to a Towards family, you might tell them (if it matches their Criteria) that this house *is close* to the schools, *has lots* of room and *is near* public transport. For an Away From family, you could say that it *isn't far* from the schools, *isn't too small* and you *don't have to walk miles* to get to public transport.

One real estate agent who studied and used the LAB Profile found that he only had to work two-thirds of the year to keep his income at the level he wanted, and this during a recessionary period when many agents had been forced to leave the business.

Culture

The LAB Profile is a tool that will enable you to understand cultures, corporate or national. One of the questions that has preoccupied Canadians for many years is: "How specifically are we different from Americans?" America, as a culture is Toward. (Remember that culture is an umbrella; any given individual may or may not fall under that umbrella.) In Europe, Americans are perceived as extremely naive, because they just go ahead and do things, while disregarding the possible negative implications. While I was living in France, during the 1980's, I did some work for the OECD (The Organization for Economic Co-operation and Development) and UNESCO (The United Nations Educational, Scientific and Cultural Organization). The criticism I heard many times about Americans within those organizations was that "They always think that just because it's a good idea, we should just go ahead and do it. They don't seem to understand that there is this political consideration and that possible problem, etc." You may recall that the American government withdrew from UNESCO.

Canadians, on the other hand are more Away From, as a culture. We do not want to rock the boat or create waves. And look at my own Jewish culture. Any group that posts a slogan of "Never Again" and prescribes chicken soup because "it couldn't hurt" has to be Away From.

SUMMARY

DIRECTION

Toward: Motivated to achieve or attain goals.

Away From: Motivated to solve or avoid problems.

Distribution: 40% mainly Away From
20% equally Toward and Away From
40% mainly Toward, in the work *Context*

INFLUENCING LANGUAGE

Toward: Attain; obtain; have; get; include; achieve, etc.

Away From: Avoid; prevent; eliminate; solve; get rid of, etc.

The Margaret Thatchers of the World: Motivation Source

> Where does the person find motivation? In external sources, or in internal standards and beliefs?

This category deals with the source of motivation, or in other words, its location. Where are judgements made; inside a person's body or from outside? These patterns affect how you make judgements and decisions. As you try them out, you will be able to decide how best to use them and others will notice your increased effectiveness.

Here are the two patterns:

Internal

People with an Internal pattern in a given context provide their own motivation from within themselves. They decide about the quality of their work. They have difficulty accepting other people's opinions and outside direction. When they get negative feedback on work they feel has been well done, they will question the opinion or judge the person giving the feedback.

They are motivated to gather *information* from outside sources and then *they decide* about it, based on internal standards. Because they take *orders as information*, they can be hard to supervise. "My boss wants this out by Tuesday? That's interesting."

Since they do not need external praise, they tend not to give much feedback as managers.

Internal people hold standards somewhere within themselves, for the things that are important to them. Their motivation is triggered when they get to gather information from the outside, process it against their own standards, and make judgements about it.

External

External people need other people's opinions, outside direction and feedback from external sources to stay motivated. In the Context of work, if they do not get that feedback, they will not know how well they are doing. They take information as orders. "He said the green paper matches the decor. I'd better go get some."

They are motivated when someone else decides. They have trouble starting or continuing an activity without outside feedback of some kind.

External people do not hold standards within themselves. They gather them from the outside. In the absence of external feedback, they will experience something akin to sensory deprivation.

DISTRIBUTION

(*in the work Context, from Rodger Bailey*)

Internal	Equally Internal/External	External
40%	20%	40%

Pattern Recognition

QUESTION: HOW DO YOU KNOW THAT YOU HAVE DONE A GOOD JOB? (at work, at choosing a car, etc.)

Internal—sentence structure

- they decide or know themselves, "I know"
- they evaluate their own performance based on their own standards and Criteria
- they resist when someone tells them what to do, or decides for them
- outside instructions are taken as information

Internal—body language

sitting upright, pointing to self, may pause before answering a judgement from someone else while they evaluate it, minimal gestures and facial expressions for their culture

External—sentence structure

- other people or external sources of information decide or judge for them
- need to compare their work to an external norm or standard i.e., a checklist or a quota
- outside information is taken as a decision or order

External—body language

leaning forward, watching for your response, facial expressions indicating they want to know from you if it was alright

Examples

Internal: "I know when I have done a good job."
Mainly Internal:
      "I usually know. I appreciate it when my boss compliments me, but generally, I know when I have done well."
Equally Internal and External:
      "Sometimes I know and sometimes my clients tell me."
Mainly External:
      "Usually, when I meet the quotas set by my boss and my clients seem happy. And also I can tell when I am working well."
External: "My clients are happy. My boss is happy. I met my quota."

Alternate Questions:

- How would you react to regular feedback from peers in (a specific Context)?
- Whom do you involve when you make a decision?
- If you felt you had done good work and someone you respect criticized your work, how would you react?

Listen if the person criticises, judges, or attempts to persuade the other person, (Internal), or if they question the value of their own work, (External).

Questioning and testing:

Here are some examples to show you how to test if you are not sure from the answer to the first question:

SRC: Can I ask you Suzanne, how do you know you've done a good job at work?

S: Feedback from other people plus knowing myself. (External & Internal)

This is an example of someone with both patterns. Because we know that only about 20% are right in the middle, I would like to test to see if Suzanne falls on one side or the other.

SRC: Let's say you thought you did a good job on something and you didn't get good feedback from the other people. How would you react?

S: Well, I'd still THINK I did a good job but . . . something would be missing. I'd have to go check what they didn't like.

Here are two more examples:

SRC: Louise, how do you know you've done a good job at work?

L: I feel good about it.

SRC: What happens if you feel good about it and nobody else appreciated it?

L: They probably didn't see what I saw in it. (shrugging her shoulders)

SRC: Robert, how do you know you've done a good job at work?

R: I know I've done a good job when I get external feedback.

SRC: What happens when there is no external feedback?

R: I would feel, like, what's the point?

While Suzanne has both patterns at work, she has more External than Internal, because, when push comes to shove, she needs the feedback to really know if it is good enough. Both Louise and Robert fall firmly in the Internal and External camps, respectively.

Where Do You Know That?

I recently discovered another question which will help you test in those cases where the answer to the first question is unclear. Ask: "*Where do you know that?*" An Internal person will point to a part of their body and an External person will not understand the question.

Other Contexts

I have worked with many groups in which there are quite a few men with a highly Internal pattern. One of them will often voice his conviction that he is always Internal because how else could one run one's life? I ask: "How do you know you bought the right suit?" The answer frequently is: "Because my wife liked it."

Someone in a training group said to me, "Well it seems to me this External stuff is really immature. Obviously, when you grow up and gain a certain amount of maturity, you become more Internal." This is a typically Internal thing to say. Let's consider another possibility. Someone who has been highly Internal, might define maturity as the ability to take other people seriously by responding to what they say they need. Instead of KNOWING what is best for them. It depends on where you are coming from and what you are trying to achieve, whether it is more appropriate to be in an Internal mode or an External mode, or both.

Margaret Thatcher

When the Commonwealth countries were negotiating about whether to impose sanctions against South Africa during its long Apartheid period, the vote was 49 countries in favour of sanctions to one against. Who was the holdout? The United Kingdom. Who specifically? Margaret Thatcher. When the vote was announced she declared: "I feel sorry for the other 49." Margaret Thatcher is an *off-the-scale* Internal.

Brian Mulroney, Michael Wilson, the GST and Free Trade

I believe that the LAB Profile can help us understand what happened when the conservative government in Canada under Brian Mulroney brought in the very unpopular Goods and Services Tax (GST). Finance Minister Michael Wilson initiated the GST and originally announced in 1990 that it was to be levied at nine percent. Who lowered it to seven percent? The Prime Minister, Brian Mulroney. How could this happen? Wouldn't you suppose that when a finance minister announces a new tax, he has the support of the prime minister?

Michael Wilson has a strong Toward and Internal combination. He had calculated, that in order to meet his goals, he needed the GST to be set at nine percent. The Canadian public vociferously rebelled at the thought of a new tax during a difficult economic period. And how did Michael Wilson respond? He expressed some regret that the public was upset but insisted that the nine percent was needed to meet his targets.

When the fury escalated, Brian Mulroney intervened over Mr. Wilson's head and lowered the tax to seven percent. Mr. Mulroney has a combination of Away From and External patterns, which means that he is motivated to respond to outside negative feedback. As Prime Minister he was well-known for *governing by opinion poll,* jumping into action whenever specific groups yelled loud enough. (I suspect that President Clinton also has this pattern.)

This pattern combination also explains Mr. Mulroney's behaviour in the summer of 1992 regarding the negotiations on the Charlottetown Constitutional Accords. While Mr. Mulroney was away in Europe, the provincial premiers came to a preliminary agreement with Joe Clark, who was representing the federal government. As a result of negative public reaction to the agreement, he vetoed it upon his return to Canada.

Who oversaw the Canadian negotiations for the North American Free Trade Agreement (NAFTA)? Mr. Michael Wilson, who by this time had become the trade minister. With his combination of Internal and Toward, he neglected to foresee potential problems in the agreement, in spite of the warnings which came from both commentators and advocacy groups. An important omission in the final agreement was the creation of a fair and timely dispute resolution mechanism.

Since the agreement came into effect, there have been many long, drawn out, high level conflicts between Canadian and American producers of steel, softwood lumber, durham wheat and beer. I often wonder if the Minister had been slightly less Internal and more Away From, whether some of these problems could have been avoided.

Making Criticism and Responding to Feedback

When an External person receives criticism or negative feedback, they question themselves. An Internal person, in the same situation, makes a judgement about the other person. "I must have done something wrong" (External) or "the customer is a jerk because he didn't appreciate what I did for him" (Internal).

If 10 people say to a highly Internal person: "Boy, is your tie ugly!" he will say "Gee isn't that funny? There are 10 people walking around here with bad taste." An External person would go home and change.

I had the advantages of being External driven home to me recently. I bought a "cheap" bookcase, in a kit, which I had to assemble myself. As I was struggling to follow the instructions (My father used to say that if all else fails, read the instructions), I noticed that the top and bottom shelves did not fit properly onto the back board. "Cheap design," I grumbled to myself and kept hammering away. When I set the bookcase up I noticed that I had assembled the top and bottom shelves backwards and the chipboard was showing! Had I been slightly more External (which is appropriate in Contexts one knows little about), I might have *questioned what I was doing* when I noticed the poor fit, instead of *criticizing the design.*

I learnt that when following instructions, it may be more appropriate to be in an External mode. My twin brother confirmed this to me when we were discussing how the holes often seem to be in the wrong place in these sort of kits; that is until you figure out that *you* made the mistake!

Recently when I returned to Paris to do some work, I went out to supper with a friend. She suggested a restaurant where she had liked both the food and the ambiance. "Although," she said," I've heard it's been taken over by new management, and that it's not nearly as good now." She then went on to insist that we go there anyway because she had to go see *for herself.* At the end of the evening she pronounced," Well, they were right; the service is poor and so was the food. But I had to check it out for myself." Being highly Internal, someone else's word was not good enough. It remained an unresolved issue for her until she could decide for herself.

Many women tell me that their husbands often do not believe them when they tell them that there is something wrong with the car. The husbands need to find out for themselves.

The easiest way to get an Internal person to listen and think about something is to phrase it as "information you might want to consider," otherwise they will simply judge you or the way you said it.

Influencing Language
You might want to consider choosing your words carefully, based on the information you have gathered about someone. As the most skilled professional communicators can tell you, the impact will be enormous.

Internal
only you can decide; you might consider; it's up to you; I suggest you think about; try it out and decide what you think; here's some information so you can decide; what do you think?; for all the information you need to decide, just . . .

External
you'll get good feedback; others will notice; it has been approved by; well-respected; you will make quite an impact; so and so thinks; I would strongly recommend; the experts say; give references

What Self-Esteem Is Not

Someone asked me a question about these patterns. "Is it possible for a person to switch from Internal to External, or vice versa, depending on whether he or she receives positive or negative criticism?" As Rodger Bailey, the developer of the LAB Profile, said: The LAB Profile is a status report about how I (with my particular structural makeup), respond to Contexts." In a few of the profiles I have done, I have noticed a pattern that corresponds to the question above. One person was highly Internal when she thought she had done a bad job (one Context) and highly External when she thought she had done something well (a different Context for her). Nothing anyone would say could convince her that she had done a good job when she had decided otherwise. However, when she thought she had done something well, she had to check with others to make sure it was alright. I suspect that this has to do with low self-esteem and self-confidence. I would this call it a self-handicapping strategy.

You should not, however, confuse an External pattern with low self-esteem. It is not the same thing. When I am presenting to a group, for example, where do I get my motivational energy from? Do I get it because the participants are smiling at me, or because I know I prepared my course well? (In that Context, if my goal is to present well and meet the audience's needs, it is appropriate to do some of each.)

A friend of mine once asked me: "Do you think I'm too External?" She then realized what she had said and began to laugh. My response was: "Too External for what?"

Educational Design

I was working with a large group of high school principals in the province of New Brunswick and we were discussing the design of education programs. One of the participants made the comment that many of the new programs are structured to create an Internal pattern in the students. In my opinion, when you closely examine the structure and content of any educational program, you could probably do a profile of its creator. Most programs will favour one or the other pattern in each of the categories. The Principal's question was: "What about the kids who have an External pattern in school and therefore need outside feedback to stay motivated and to know if they are doing well?"

I believe that it is fine to teach and encourage self-evaluation. However, when you want to *trigger motivation and keep the students interested* (which is a separate Context), some people will need on-going feedback or results to stay interested.

Hiring

Does the job need someone who must *provide their own motivation and judge for themselves* the quality of their work? Or does it need someone to *adapt what they are doing based on outside requirements?* Sales and reception positions, or any job where meeting someone else's needs is crucial, generally need someone with an External pattern. You would want to employ someone in these positions for whom feedback will determine what they do and how they behave. These people will need to be closely supervised, or have some external means of knowing if they are on track.

Many people management positions require someone who is mainly Internal with some External. Managers make decisions and set standards. You would have to have standards inside your body somewhere to do that. Frequently people say, however, when their boss is extremely Internal, that he or she does not listen or respond to suggestions.

For sales positions, you would need a good dose of External. In today's market, sales people must inherently care whether customers are happy. If a customer is not pleased with your product or service and your representative explains that it is because the customer is a jerk, it would not help you improve customer service. One of the challenges that large Internal organizations have is how to incorporate customer feedback into product development and design.

However, one of the latest currents in sales concerns promoting the salesperson as a *long term partner and consultant* to clients. If your sales representatives do consulting, that presupposes that they have some expertise to impart, for example, on technical issues and standards. The salesperson / consultant would therefore need to have some degree of Internal. You would not however want someone who is overly Internal because their performance is ultimately judged by the satisfaction of the client.

When you are profiling a job in preparation for hiring or selection, you will need to determine whether the person's success at the position is based on meeting their own standards or adapting to someone else's.

People Management

Internal people have trouble accepting being managed and generally do not need praise to stay motivated. Their motivation comes from inside and they are self-starters. They need to make their own decisions and will do that even when they have not been given permission. They become demotivated when they do not get to decide anything. When you give them an instruction, they will consider that as a piece of information and then decide whether to follow it.

A friend recounted an inter-cultural incident between two Internals, an English manager, and an American employee. The English boss told his employee: "I'd reconsider that if I were you," intending to communicate that he thought it was a bad idea and it should not be done. The American took him literally; he reconsidered, decided it was a good idea, went ahead and did it, much to the annoyance of his boss.

When two or more Internal people are on a team, you can predict that they will have frequent arguments and conflicts because each will be operating from their own, usually unstated, internal standards. They can work more successfully together when they first negotiate and explicitly agree upon the standards and measurements.

Employees with an Internal pattern work best with little supervision. You can assign them a task and give them "carte blanche" to see it through. Give them decisions to make and, in cases where you are not sure of their judgement, get agreement on the standards to be met first. Make sure you know their Criteria and attach them to the job to be done. "Here's a *challenge* for you."

When giving them instructions, preface them with "Only you can decide to . . . " or "Here is the information on this, the end goal is to achieve that. You get to decide the best way."

External employees will look to their manager for guidance and encouragement. You will need to be explicit about what you expect them to do, as they tend to interpret information as instructions. If you said to an External employee: "The order forms are now available," they would drop what they were doing and go get them.

In the absence of regular feedback, they will become demotivated and unsure of themselves. Where the manager is highly External, he may end up looking to the employees for approval. External employees need to have clear goals and some external means of knowing if they are on track. This can take the form of regular feedback sessions, checklists, quotas, or examples to follow.

Annual performance appraisals are insufficient feedback for people who have an External pattern. Many will work themselves into a lather before their performance appraisal because they have *no idea* themselves of how well they have been performing.

When assigning a task to an External person, let them know how much it will be appreciated (if his or her Organization pattern is Person) or what the impact will be (if his or her Organization pattern is Thing). "You will get lots of good feedback," or "This will make a noticeable difference to our work" are phrases you could use to get their interest. The tasks that will play to their strengths are those which demand that they adapt to and meet someone else's expectations, provided that those expectations are clear.

Irresistible Language: Managing Your Boss

Some people are extremely hard to influence or convince, *until you know how*. Let's take an example of someone, perhaps your boss, who has the following combination: Internal and Away From. Chances are that this person has been making your life miserable by only noticing what you do wrong, and disagreeing with every proposal. As Groucho Marx sang, "Whatever it is, I'm against it."

So you need some *irresistible* Influencing Language, tailor-made for this person. Let's imagine that one day you enter her office with the report she asked you for and you say: "I've drafted the proposal you asked for to deal with the issues. *It's not perfect. Would you take a look at it?*" Your boss will grab the paper from your hand, correct it to her liking and accept it.

Selling in a Buyer's Market

When discussing sales and marketing, there are two axes to consider: Promoting *who you are* (your organization's image or how you are perceived) and communicating to *the people you want to reach*. It is no secret that IBM for example, has been struggling to be viewed as a more External company. They want to be perceived as giving the customer what the customer wants instead of what *they* have to offer. Their 1994 television commercial says it all: "We're trying to be more customer-focused." Trying?

You will need to decide what kind of image you want to convey. Are you the *experts* with the solutions or the company who will do what it takes to *meet your customers' needs*, or both.

There is no replacement for good market research. Canada Trust (a Canadian trust and mortgage company) seems to have responded to the change in the mortgage market. Since the early 90's there has been a buyers' market, with mortgage companies begging people to choose them. Buyers have become highly selective; in other words, Internal. So the Canada Trust slogan was highly appropriate: "The best mortgage package in Canada? You be the judge."

Burger King has also been targeting Internals (and Proactives): "Your way. Right away." McDonald's, on the other hand, decides for you what you will have on your hamburger.

The sales approach of a local career counselling outfit consisted of booking an appointment with prospective clients, showing them the process they use, and then sending the person away to think about it and decide if they needed it. Upon questioning, it turned out that about 80% of their clients had an Internal pattern. So did the founder and majority of staff. When I suggested that they *might consider* using an approach for

External people to attract more clients, the founder thought about it and decided against it. He felt that External clients would take up too much time in counselling sessions.

The national marketing director of a company that sells blood analysis equipment to hospitals spoke to me about a change in the buying process of their customers. Laboratory equipment used to be selected by the chief lab technician, who usually had a long-standing rapport with the sales representative. Now, all buying decisions are made centrally in the purchasing department. The sales reps were finding themselves confronting highly Internal purchasing officers whose Criteria were about price and who did not understand the technical aspects of the equipment. They needed to change their sales approach by matching the price Criterion, giving only relevant information (one piece of which was the approval of the equipment by the chief lab technician) and asking the purchasing officer "to be the judge."

To sell to Internals you need to give them information and let them decide. I wrote an advertisement for a management training course geared to Internals which had this statement at the bottom of the ad: "For all the information you need to decide, call ... " We had one person sign up over the phone without even bothering to find out what was in the course. We also had many calls for information that subsequently led to enrolments.

"I would like you to try it out and tell me what you think. The only way to know if this is the one for you, is to test it out for yourself." That is why car dealerships insist that their sales people get the prospective buyer behind the wheel.

In France, I read a study which pronounced that 80% of patients do not finish taking their prescriptions. Doctors have told me that about the same percentage applies in North America. Many people stop taking their medicine when their symptoms disappear. We can use the LAB Profile to explain this. Many people have Internal and Away From patterns in the Context of bodily ailments. Most people go to the doctor when they feel sick, not when someone else says they look unwell.

Doctors would therefore need to sell their patients on complying with their instructions. "*You need to decide* if you want to *get rid of this illness*. If you do, you will need to take all of this medicine, as prescribed." (Internal and Away From) Even though many people are External to doctors and other authority figures, once they get home, they shift back into an Internal mode.

This approach would also work for Internals in other Contexts. "You need to decide if you really want (*their desired outcome*). If you do, then you'll need to get (*our product or service*)."

External people need references. They need to know who else has bought. The advertisements where a famous person is flogging a product attract the attention of people who are External to that famous person, in that Context.

It can be easier selling to people provided you can get them to be External to you. This entails establishing credibility as well as rapport. One client of mine asked me: "Do you think I need it?" You can do this by wearing clothes that are one notch more formal than your client's, show credentials and references, and slip in expressions such as "In my experience" or "If I were you, knowing what I know today . . . "

External people will also buy something for how it will make them look or the impact it will have on others. Why *do* people buy Jaguars? Because the leather seats are comfortable? According to a market researcher who worked on the Jaguar account, people today buy luxury cars more for the perceived value these cars offer than the status they confer. Then he stopped and thought. "Maybe," he said, "they are buying because they want to *be seen* as buying for value."

If you want to attract both groups, or if your client pays attention to internal standards and external feedback, use both patterns. For those cases where you are not sure, use one pattern and observe. If you do not get a positive response, try the other one.

SUMMARY

SOURCE

Internal: They are motivated to decide based on their own internal standards.

External: They need outside feedback to know how well they are doing and to stay motivated.

Distribution: 40% mainly Internal
20% equally Internal and External
40% mainly External

INFLUENCING LANGUAGE

Internal: Only you can decide; you might want to consider; it's up to you; what do you think?, etc.

External: Others will notice; the feedback you'll get; results; give references; so and so thinks, etc.

Sometimes You Just Gotta Break the Rules: Motivation Reason

> How does a person reason? Is there a continual quest to find alternatives, or is there a preference to follow established procedures?

This category will lead you to unlimited possibilities and show you the right way to get there. There are two patterns:

Options

Options people are motivated by opportunities and possibilities to do something in a different way. There is always another better way to do things. They love to create procedures and systems but have great difficulty following them. If you give an Options person a guaranteed way to make a million dollars, they will try to improve it.

They are thrilled by unlimited possibilities and ideas. The thing that is totally irresistible to Options people is breaking or bending the rules.

Options people like to start a new idea or a new project. However, they do not necessarily feel compelled to finish it. They much prefer to do development and set up rather than maintenance activities. Sometimes they will have difficulty committing themselves because they believe this will reduce their options. At the extreme, they might avoid deciding anything (particularly if they are also Reactive). Alternatively, they can be totally committed to an idea or project, until the next new idea comes along.

Procedures

Procedures people like to follow set ways. They believe there is a "right" way to do things. Once they have a procedure they can follow it over and over again. These are people who are interested in how to do things, *not in why* things are the way they are.

A procedure has a beginning and an end. It may have choice points in which you gather more information and make a decision. Without one, Procedure people feel lost or get stuck. When they commence a procedure, the most important thing for them is to get to the end of the procedure. They are the ones who will complete and finish what they start.

Procedures people feel personally violated when it is suggested to them to break, or go around the rules. Once they know the procedure to follow, they are happy doing that.

DISTRIBUTION

(in the work Context, from Rodger Bailey)

Equally

Options	Options & Procedures	Procedures
40%	20%	40%

Pattern Recognition

QUESTION: WHY DID YOU CHOOSE YOUR PRESENT JOB?
(or house, vacation, car, etc.)

You may recall that, in the introduction of this book, we discussed Reality. In order for people to create their own models of reality, they use three processes called Deletion, Distortion and Generalization. This category deals with Distortion. The question we ask for this pattern is: "Why did you choose . . . " and the rest refers to a particular Context.

For Options people, when they hear the question **Why did you choose?**, they hear the question why and give you a list of Criteria for their answer.

When Procedures people hear the question, they delete the word why and substitute **how did it come to be?** They answer the question: "How?" Sometimes, the first thing they will say is, "Well I didn't choose." They will tell you a story or series of events that led them to getting the job. "I was working at my brother-in-law's and there was an opening in this other company at the time I finished a contract, so I took it."

Options
- list of Criteria
- opportunities, possibilities
- expanding options and choice

Procedures

- did not choose
- answers the question "why" by telling "how" it came to pass
- the facts, events leading to, a story

How you recognize someone who is equally Options and Procedures is interesting. They might tell you a story with Criteria imbedded in it. I happen to be quite in the middle on this pattern, and if someone asked me why I chose to set up my own company after I came back to Canada, I would say: "I was working in another company for a while when I came back and I wasn't **happy**. And **being organized** is important to me. I realized that I could probably make **more money** on my own, and **decrease expenses** and **be independent**. So I set up my company, Success Strategies." I have used both patterns throughout the answer.

Examples

Options:

"I thought it would be stimulating, interesting and a challenge."

Mainly Options:

"It was more interesting, had more responsibility, and better pay. A friend of mine told me about it."

Equally Options and Procedures:

"A friend told me about it and it looked more interesting."

Mainly Procedures:

"I had been with the same company ten years. A friend told me they were hiring in her company, so I applied and was hired. The job is more interesting and I make more money."

Procedures:

"I didn't really choose. I met my boss through my brother-in-law who worked with her. They needed a technician and I was just completing a contract."

Alternate Question:

What would your typical work day be like?
(listen for Criteria or a set of procedures to be followed)
Note: Make sure you ask "*Why* did you choose?" and *not* "*How* did you choose?"

Influencing Language

The possibilities are endless for finding the right thing to say.

Options

- opportunity; choice; break the rules just for you; another better way; unlimited possibilities; an alternative is; that's one way; here are the options; there has got to be a way; the sky's the limit

Procedures

- the right way; speak in procedures: first . . . then . . . after which . . . the last step; tried and true; reliable; how to use this; just follow the procedure; the procedure is; proven methodology

Hiring

You can see that for hiring, the Options and Procedures patterns are quite important. In fact, this is one category where it really pays to get it right. When you profile a position, you will need to ask yourself, does the job mainly consist of *following procedures* or is it about *creating and designing systems and procedures*? Is it set up and development or maintenance? When you know what the balance is, you can write your advertisement to attract the right people and turn off the ones who would not fit. (See also the section on writing advertisements for jobs.)

You may have heard of some of the multi-level marketing companies or MLM's, such as NSA, Mary Kay, Nu Skin, and a number of other products. They have a real problem. Only one person in ten on average succeeds at making a full-time living at multi-level sales. I would say that this is very poor statistics for hiring, wouldn't you?

In my opinion, the reason is in how they promote themselves. The multi-level marketing companies try to recruit new distributors by telling them about *unlimited income possibilities*. This is Options language. Things with unlimited choice or possibilities, or no ceilings or the sky's the limit, are *irresistible* to Options people.

However, when people actually become distributors they usually find that the companies have already worked out the procedures for selling the product. All you have to do is proactively and consistently follow the procedure to make your *sky's the limit* income, which most of them are incapable of doing. The irony is that if they used Procedures Influencing Language in their promotional packages, recruits would indeed make their unlimited income.

According to Rodger Bailey, there has also been some research done on telemarketers, and this would apply to other kinds of salespeople.

Telemarketers who have a Procedures pattern sell three times as much as the Options people. The reason for this is simple. Sales is basically a procedure. You contact prospective customers, establish rapport, do a needs analysis, present something that matches the needs and lastly you help the person make a decision. That's a procedure. If I am an Options person this time I will do it one way. Another time I will try another way. Options sales people tend to have an up and down performance, because occasionally they will get a brilliant idea and strike gold. They do not, however hone their procedure until it works well. Procedures people will continue to follow the same process over and over again because it feels comfortable and right. This is ideal for sales. Although in changing sales situations, they would need to be taught a new procedure.

Certain kinds of jobs are inherently Options or Procedures. Flying an airplane, for example, is quite clearly a procedure. Can you imagine a commercial airline pilot who has an Options pattern? "Let's go over the North Pole this time." Anything to do with safety and security needs a Procedures person. Emergency procedures need to memorized and followed to the letter. Someone who is Internal and Procedures would do very well at that kind of work. On the other hand, you would want an Options person to develop and test a safety procedure, preferably one who also has an Away From pattern to avoid mistakes.

Architecture would need someone with lots of Options and an understanding of Procedures. A building contractor would have a much heavier dose of Procedures to ensure compliance to regulations. You might want to test for this if you are going to do renovations.

Options people excel in situations where there is a need to develop creative solutions, or alternatives to the present systems. Business process engineers, for example, would need a heavy dose of Options.

In a training company in France, I worked closely with my boss who has high Options and Internal patterns in his work. I learned much from him about creative seminar design. We frequently were asked to lead the same seminar several times over in the same large organizations. We would meet before each one to prepare and he would insist that we redesign each one. I would object: "But Pierre, it worked well last time, it was really good and they liked it." He would say: "No, no, there has to be a better way to do this." I had the feeling we were constantly throwing the baby out with the bath water. You can see the conflict between Options and Procedures people.

In fact, to design training you need to have Options, but in order to perfect the delivery of training you need to have enough Procedures to be able to repeat processes that work. The best public speakers have well-honed routines, which necessitates both Options and Procedures.

A Little Variety

For many years there has been a crisis in nursing. The media occasionally discuss examples of this from several European countries as well as in North America. It is not solely attributed to low wages and abusive treatment by other medical professions. When I ask nurses: "Why did you choose to become a nurse?", the answer often is something like: "I want to help people.", or "Once I got my certificate, I could travel." These are Criteria, Options answers. Many people who are attracted to nursing are interested because of the *possibilities* nursing has to offer. They are Options people. After they decide to become nurses, they go to nursing college. Who teaches in the nursing schools? People who did not find what they wanted in hospital work. So, the nursing students get their certificates and go to work in the hospitals. What are hospitals all about? Procedures, and often very tight ones with little choice.

Now, in North America at least, where there is an increasing emphasis on home-based care, we have an expanding number of private nursing services. You can be a nurse, care for people and do it your own way, getting a chance to develop alternatives. Hospitals themselves are also changing. One hospital I did some work for is well in advance of the trend in creating "Patient Care Teams", which include many of the medical professionals. This is a more Options approach to patient care.

In order to attract people who will perform well and be fulfilled by traditional hospital nursing, they should be producing promotional materials that say: "Do you want to practice medicine the right way? Learn patient care from start to finish."

Culture Clashes at Work

One of the things I have noticed when participating in change operations in corporations is the internal culture clash between different departments. Let's take software design and marketing, for example. If you are a software designer, chances are you have a mainly Options pattern. You develop and design software. Marketing tends to be mainly Procedures because there are procedures to follow to take the product to market. The software designers develop some software and often they drop one project to work on another. They will keep changing it and adapting it and making it better and coming up with alternative solutions. The marketing department will be screaming at them "Stop fixing it! Just give it to us so we can get it out on the market." Why are there so many upgrades to your favourite software package? A consultant friend summed up the software problem: "Not enough time to do it right once, but all the time in the world to fix it."

The same thing happens between the design engineers and the plant.

Terminal Options

The Latest Revision!

What do those engineers do? They create systems and design products. What does the plant do? It makes them. Production managers get furious when engineering keeps changing the specs.

In order to work more effectively together and reduce the number of conflicts between Options and Procedures departments, each needs to understand the role of the other and how they function. Options people need to creatively explore possibilities in order to invent solutions. The Procedures people need to know that the fruit of these deliberations will actually arrive completed at the right time and place. Many companies would do well to have a person who is equally Options and Procedures co-ordinating the work between these two.

Sales and Marketing

The means of choice for selling to an Options person is to get them to think of the possibilities. Give them lots of alternatives. They want to examine all the reasons *why* they should buy. I remember having a sales appointment with someone who was grappling with a problem. As I left, I inadvertently used an irresistible pattern. I said "There's gotta be a way to find what you're looking for." By the time I had returned to my office, the phone was ringing off the hook. She said: " You're right. There's gotta be a way. And you're the one who can help me." An Options person is motivated by unlimited choice. The more choice the better. To close the sale irresistibly, break with the normal procedure, just for them. My carpet cleaner told me: "The office says we have to charge $50, but since I'm already here, I can do that for you for $30."

If you want to know the right way to sell to a Procedures person, there are two keys. One is to get them started on a procedure because they are compelled to finish it and the other one is to have them understand that this product or service is the tried and true, right way to do things. They will be more interested in *how* to buy it or how to use it than why they should buy it.

"The first step is, I'll show you how we have laid out these products. Then you can look at the merchandise and try it out. After that I'll tell you about the payment plan and we can choose which one will fit your needs and set it up for you to sign, and lastly, you can take your product home right away." You will have already started them on the first part of the procedure. If the product meets their Criteria, (and other factors do not interfere), they will complete the procedure. It is preferable to have the client going away happy with the product as the last step of the procedure, rather than paying the bill as the last step.

Certain kinds of stores naturally attract one or the other pattern. Some people, me for example, are overwhelmed by the large amount of choice one has in music stores. Others are thrilled.

A well-known home furnishings chain which imports Far Eastern rattan furniture, cotton fabrics with Asian prints, etc., ran an advertising campaign in magazines with an image on a grid pattern. A grid is a Procedures image. According to Rodger Bailey, with this ad they increased their floor traffic by 20%. However 75% of the people who came in because of the ad, came into the store only once, and never came back. Why? It attracted Procedures people, but what does the store actually look like? It has clusters of stuff over here, clusters of stuff over there. It is very Options, lots of choice, all kinds of different materials, all kinds of gadgets, bricabrac, etc. A consultant looked at the results and a new advertisement was designed. This time they laid out the ad in the same way the stores are laid out. Clusters of images. They had another increase in store traffic and a much higher percentage of the people who came in came back more than once.

Let's compare that chain to IKEA, the Swedish home furnishings, put it together yourself, store. When you walk into IKEA you cannot get out until you have gone through the entire store, (short of pulling the fire alarm). I know, I have tried. They have a procedure for doing everything. They have procedures for walking through the store, measuring, deciding, ordering, lining up, paying, parking, loading and assembling the furniture once you get home.

Different Contexts create buying patterns among large groups of people. In the Context of buying cars, a large percentage of the population has an Options pattern, concerning the car company and the model they choose. They might want a Ford Taurus or a Honda Civic and they will tell you why. They are motivated by Criteria when they choose the make and model. Why did you choose your car? Because it has good fuel efficiency? Because it has great pick up? Because there isn't another one like on the road? Or some other Criteria? Probably not because you were walking along the street one day when you needed a car and happened to see one.

However, in the Context of choosing a dealership, most people have a Procedures pattern. This means they do not have Criteria about what dealership they choose. The first one they stumble on will do. For example, that is why all the Ford dealers in your region sponsor commercials together on local television stations. They know that which dealership you go to is of no importance, unless you experience very bad service and never want to go back there again.

Let's take fast food chains again. When someone buys a McDonald's franchise, they find it is a turn key operation. All the procedures are in place.

The products are Procedures as well. When you get a Big Mac it is always a Big Mac and it is always done the same way. The *right way*.

Compare them to Burger King one more time. Burger King's slogan in 1992 was: "Sometimes you just gotta break the rules." Now look at the Burger King products. You can have tomato or not, onions or not, relish and mustard or not, etc. Options. Their 1993 slogan was: " Your way. Right Away." It is appealing to Proactive, Internal, Options people (in the Context of eating at fast food places). I am willing to bet that their clientele has a different Profile than McDonald's. It has little to do with how their products taste. How different can one beef or chicken pattie be from another?

People Management

Options people work best in situations where they get to develop or set up new systems and procedures. They will invariably find a way around standard operating procedures, so you will need to decide how best to harness their creativity. They will be motivated by tasks that involve creating something from scratch, particularly where the end result will increase options. To motivate them, you can tell them to think of the possibilities or to find an alternative to what we do now.

You can motivate Procedures people by telling them that this is the *right way* to do something. They feel comfortable doing the same thing over and over. Let them know how important the finished result is.

For staff who are Equally Options and Procedures at work, you will need to give them the opportunity to both follow and develop or improve the procedures. You can use the Influencing Language for both patterns. "You will get to develop a better way to do this. Make sure it is right (Internal and Procedures), and then you can use it from now on." For someone who is External, you could substitute: "Check with me to make sure it is right . . ."

Total Quality Management?

Many organizations have been preoccupied with introducing Total Quality Management, Continuous Improvement programs and other forms of paradigm shifting. They are aiming to get employees into new ways of thinking in order to respond to environments that are constantly changing. What are these programs designed to create? Options. Basically the message is to tell workers that they ought to be Options people. You ought to be able to turn on a dime, totally change what you are doing, develop alternatives, create new systems to anticipate and respond to environmental changes.

What would actually happen to the corporate world, the helping professions, the education system or any other sector if no one finished or completed procedures? Imagine that for a moment. The new management practices have been designed to tell whole groups of people that what they do is no good, and yet if procedures were not completed, no money would be made.

I have found many biases against the idea of the Procedures pattern. My colleagues in France who teach the LAB profile found that they had to change the terminology. Instead of using the word *Procedures*, they changed it to *Process*. They found such a negative association with *being procedural* that people would not accept the term. And this, in the country that invented the word *bureaucracy*.

I believe it is important to honour Procedures people for what they contribute instead of pointing out to them how rigid this makes them. They get things done. We need Options people to think of new options, and we need Procedures people to see that they get done. Building a high performance team depends on how well you use the strengths in the team to accomplish what needs to be done.

Learning New Skills

Learning is a specific Context. People have different learning styles and knowing your Profile in that Context (or that of the people you are teaching) is useful for accelerating the speed at which new material can be integrated.

Why Some of Us Can't Understand Computer Nerds

A few years ago I got my first computer. I had quite a few different packages of software with it. The person from whom I bought it was an experienced computer user and he spent quite a lot of time teaching me. He would say, "I'd like you to *understand why* it's set up this way." I would say: "No, I don't want to understand why it's set up this way. Tell me *how* to turn it on." "Well," he would continue, "You need to *understand a few of the concepts* behind this particular program." "No I don't. I want to know *how you make* and *print* a document." Or he would say in response to a how-to question: "There are *several ways* you can do this." And I would answer, feeling my blood pressure rise: "I don't want to know several ways. Just tell me *one way. The right way!*"

I needed the procedure to follow. It was only after I had mastered some needed procedures that I was the least bit interested in why things were set up the way they were. In that circumstance he could have matched my style by telling me: "I'm going to show you the *basic procedure* for making and printing a document. Once you've got that down, I'll explain *how it* works so that you can master the other things you'll need to do. Then *you will be able* to figure it out for yourself." An Options person would be motivated by all the possibilities the software has to offer. However, I suspect that many computer neophytes, and others learning new skills, simply want the procedure to follow.

Who writes the manuals for all your software and your computer? Options people, generally speaking. That is one possible explanation for why I, like many others, have difficulty understanding the manuals. The vocabulary is another problem. An exception is the very popular "For Dummies" series of manuals. They give you the step-by-step procedure and even warn you when they are about to give you some "technical drivel."

When you are learning or teaching something, it is useful to assess whether the need is to know the why's and wherefore's or to simply know how to.

Working With Groups

When you are giving instructions to a group, if you give them options they will be paralysed. You must be procedural when giving instructions to a group or they will not know what to do. I was giving an introductory workshop on the LAB Profile at a conference in Montreal and we did not finish all the patterns we wanted to do in the allotted time. The group seemed frustrated and wanted to continue. I said, "Okay, well there are some options. We could break for lunch now and come back early and do the last pattern, or we could keep going now and have lunch later, or we could just forget it. What would you prefer?" Everybody went um, ah, um. No answer. I said "I have a suggestion. Let's break for lunch now. Those of you who want to, can come back a half an hour early and we'll meet in this room and we'll do it." They said great, and everyone left for lunch.

When explaining an exercise or assigning a task to a group, you need to explicitly give them the step-by-step procedure.

Coaching and Counselling

When we are coaching or counselling people, we often try to help them have more choice about what they do. If you have a Procedures person and you give him too many choices, you may inadvertently put him into sensory overload. Not deprivation, overload. Too much choice. What people with a Procedures pattern need is a procedure to enable them to discover what they want.

SUMMARY

REASON

Options: Compelled to develop and create systems and procedures. Have difficulty following set procedures.

Procedures: Prefer to follow tried and true set ways. Get stumped when they have no procedures to follow.

Distribution: 40% mainly Options
20% equally Options and Procedures
40% mainly Procedures

INFLUENCING LANGUAGE

Options: Opportunities; variety; unlimited possibilities; lots of choice; options; break the rules just for them

Procedures: The right way; how to; tried and true; speak in procedures: first . . . then . . . lastly

When the Bell Tolls:
Motivation Decision Factors

> How does a person react to change and what frequency of change is needed? Does the motivation come from a search for "difference" or "sameness?"

The Decision Factors category is about your internal time clock and how often the *bell rings* for change. Are you motivated by evolution, revolution, both or stability? There are four patterns:

Sameness

Sameness people want their situation in a given Context to stay the same. They do not like change and may refuse to adapt. They may accept a major change once every ten years, but they will provoke change only once every *15 to 25 years*.

Sameness With Exception

Sameness with Exception people like a given Context to stay mainly the same but will accept change once a year, if the change is not too drastic. They prefer their situations to evolve slowly over time. They tend to resist major changes except when they are perceived to be progressive or gradual. They need major change once every *five to seven years*. This is by far the largest category in the work Context and probably in many other Contexts.

Difference

People with a Difference pattern love change; they thrive on it and want it to be constant and major. They will resist static or stable situations. They need drastic change about every *one to two years*, and if they do not get it, they may leave. They like change to be revolutionary, dramatically different.

Sameness With Exception and Difference (the double pattern)

People with this double pattern like change and revolutionary shifts but are also comfortable where things are evolving. They are happy with both revolution and evolution. They need major change every *three to four years*, on average.

DISTRIBUTION			
(in the work Context, from Rodger Bailey)			
Sameness	Sameness with Exception	Difference	Sameness with Exception and Difference
5%	65%	20%	10%

Pattern Recognition

QUESTION: WHAT IS THE RELATIONSHIP BETWEEN YOUR WORK THIS YEAR AND LAST YEAR? (vacation, this home and the last one, etc.)

or

WHAT IS THE RELATIONSHIP BETWEEN THIS JOB AND YOUR LAST ONE?

The question asks: "What is the relationship between . . . ?" In this framework, the word *relationship* has the connotation of similarity. People will either naturally understand the word and tell you how it is the same or similar, or alternatively they will not know what you mean or reinterpret it to mean how is it *different*.

Sameness
- how they are the same, identical
- what they have in common
- how it has not changed

Sameness with Exception
- how is has evolved over time
- it is the same except more; less; better; worse; improving; etc. (comparisons on a sliding scaler)
- focus on the trip more than arriving at the destination

Difference
- doesn't understand the word *relationship*
- will describe how it is completely different
- new, different, changed, transformed, revolutionary
- language points to an immediate switch
- focus on the destination, ignore the trip

Difference and Sameness with Exception
- use *both* Difference and Sameness with Exception language

Examples

Sameness: "It is exactly the *same*. I'm *still* crunching numbers."
Sameness with exception:
"It's the *same but* I have *more* responsibility and *less* time."
Difference: "It's *totally different*. Now I do outside sales."
Difference and Sameness with Exception:
"There have been *big changes* this year and my performance has *improved greatly*."

To test your diagnosis in the work context, simply ask the person how often they changed what they were doing on the job. They may have had the same job title, but what we are looking for is *how often* they changed responsibilities. Their answers will usually match the change clocks for their pattern. In other Contexts you could check by asking how often they have moved homes, what they do for a vacation each year; do they go to the same cottage or do different things, etc.

You will need to be especially clear in identifying the Context when you ask the question because peoples' patterns often change depending upon what they are talking about. I profiled a man in several Contexts and regarding work he said, "Well it's *basically the same*, I have *more* responsibility, I've got *more* people to supervise and *more* accounts." Sameness with Exception. Then I said, "OK, what's the relationship between the last holiday you took and the holiday before that?" He said "Relationship! What do you mean by relationship?" Two minutes after answering the first *relationship* question he was suddenly unable to understand the word relationship, simply because we had switched Contexts.

Influencing Language

Here are some totally new ways to improve communication and maintain rapport.

Sameness
same as; in common; as you always do; like before; unchanged; as you already know; maintaining; totally the same; exactly as before; identical

Sameness with Exception
more; better; less; the same except; advanced; upgrade; progression; gradual improvement; similar but even better; moving up; growth; improvement

Difference
new; totally different; unlike anything else; unique; one of a kind; completely changed; unrecognizable; shift; switch; a complete turn around; brand new; unheard of; the only one

Sameness with Exception & Difference
use both Sameness with Exception and Difference vocabulary

Making Your Change Pattern Work For You

Since people may have different patterns from Context to Context, it is important not to make generalizations about someone. A friend of mine, while he makes frequent changes in his work, always wants to go to the same restaurant to order the same thing. People who have a Difference pattern in the Context of reading usually have four or five books on the go at any one time. Some people have cottages where they spend their vacation every year. Others would not consider going to the same place twice.

When I looked at my own history, I discovered that I have moved residences about every 18 months. I have also discovered that if you do that, banks and other financial institutions will think you are a flake. Guess what pattern they have?

Knowing your own pattern can help you to understand and predict what is happening in your life. When my change bell rang one fall, suddenly I started to notice all the things that were wrong with the place I was living. I was itching to move. I told myself that since I was working on a number of business projects and I needed co-operation from the bank, I would need them to perceive me as a steady, *normal* type. So, I had my living room painted, bought some new furniture, moved around the old stuff, and made the whole place *feel different*. After I received the needed financial backing, I cracked and bought a new place.

I have a friend who has a combination of high Options and high Difference patterns in the Contexts of work and study. She started and had not completed three different Masters programs at three universities in different cities. She adopted three children from different backgrounds.

"Hamster migration— every seven years."

After her first undergraduate degree, she went back to school and became a nurse. Every so often she would go back to hospital work because she really liked to take care of people. She would usually stay for a bit, get frustrated by the procedures, and leave. Her change pattern is an average of one to two years and for some Contexts it is as short as six months.

As a student it was very difficult for her, because if she has read a book once, she could not stand the idea of reading it again. She wanted to read something different. She did her Profile with me and decided "I'm doing this Masters program and I am finishing it." (She also has an Internal pattern.) This was the third attempt, and she managed to build in many different projects towards her Masters degree. For her thesis, she conducted some research in Asia to complete her degree, while her husband was there on sabbatical. She found a way to *build her need for Difference into her activities.*

Her husband has a Sameness with Exception pattern for several Contexts. He is interested in evolution and progression, while she prefers to have things changing all the time. How can this work in a marriage? Since none of us are actually living in Reality, who cares what your spouse's patterns may be as long as he *thinks it is getting better* and *she thinks it is totally different?* And so long as he does not bang his shins on the furniture when she moves it around.

For couples with different patterns, I would suggest that each understand their own need for change, as well as their spouse's, and make sure each feels their needs are being met.

Revolutions and Evolutions: Hiring

There are several things to think about when doing a Job Profile in preparation for hiring. Does the job require a great variety of tasks? How long does each task remain the same? Does the successful fulfilment of the objectives demand creating a revolution (Difference), building upon what is already there (Sameness with Exception), or maintaining the status quo (Sameness)? How much of each?

You can predict that people with a high Difference pattern will create revolutions around them, especially if they are also Proactive and Options. In fact, someone with a combination of Options and Difference patterns is usually a compulsive change artist. I wanted to call on a client with this pattern after not seeing him for two years. I tried the company where he had been working. He had, of course, left and gone somewhere else.

I profiled a man, and told him about his Difference pattern and what that meant for his career. He retorted that he had been a high school teacher and principal for 30 years. I asked him in how many schools had he worked? He had been in 17 *different schools*. Knowing this pattern will allow you to predict someone's past. A great party trick.

Since the majority of people (65%) in the work Context have a Sameness with Exception pattern, you will be more likely to find those candidates. Many jobs need someone who can build and progress. A fewer number of positions actually require revolutionaries.

People Management

Employees with a Sameness pattern do not respond well to change. They are well-suited to tasks that do not change, such as many administrative or production tasks. Managers with this pattern strive to keep standards up and want to provide continuity. This attribute is also appropriate for maintaining a long term rapport with clients.

To motivate Sameness employees, talk about what this task has in common with what they already know.

Sameness with Exception employees will accept change once a year as long as it is not too drastic. They will feel stressed if placed in high change environments, which explains the stress-related illnesses that are rampant in the post-recessionary nineties. They are motivated when they can perceive a *progression* in their work. To get them interested in a task you can tell them how it will make things better, or will build on what they are already doing.

I've Been Moved

To capture the interest of someone with a Difference pattern, you will need to give them lots of different things to work on. Get them to change things (if they are also Proactive) or create changes for them to respond to (if they are Reactive). For some companies this happens frequently anyway. A group of IBM European headquarters managers told me the nickname they have for IBM is "I've Been Moved". Europeans are not used to the American habit of moving people around every few years. (I also heard that the nickname given to the European headquarters of IBM was "La cage aux foils" because no one makes a presentation without overhead foils.)

Difference people will need to hear how what they are doing is totally different. Remember the line from Monty Python's Flying Circus? "And now, for something completely different."

Taking the Pain Out of Organizational Change

Once upon a time, large companies had work groups that were called typing pools. Many of the people who worked in typing pools stayed there for a long time, sometimes 15, 20 or 25 years, typing documents all day long. Then a miracle occurred. Word processors were invented. The agents of change were very excited by all the *different possibilities* these wonderful new machines could offer. They heralded the arrival of the miraculous machines by announcing to the people working in the typing pools: "We have bought some *totally new machines* which are going to *revolutionize* how you do your work." Many people resigned. Many panicked and said "I'm too old to learn this. I can't do this. I am a failure." Now typing pools have completely disappeared from the workplace.

The moral of the story has little to do with the revolutionary machines. If you had been typing for over 15 years, would you really be interested in revolution? The **language** of change created much unnecessary resistance in the workforce. Forget the word *new*. Forget the word *revolution*. A more appropriate language for populations which have Sameness and Procedures patterns would be: "We have bought some machines which are *exactly like* a typewriter. They have the *same* keyboard. They have a *few* extra keys which allow you to go *faster*, work *better*, correct mistakes *easier*, but *essentially*, *they're the same*. And we'll *teach you the procedure* for using them."

From the mid 1980's to the early 1990's, organizations began to notice that large numbers of their workforce balked at frequent changes. Many introduced "Continuous Improvement" programs. They were not called "Dramatic Difference" programs.

The introduction of workstations, personal and networked computers, and statistical process control on the shop floor was (and is) often mishandled in the same way. It is important to prepare the ground work for major technological and organizational changes. Knowing your workforce and planning your announcements and implementation, by matching the language you use with the people affected, can *dramatically improve* the chances of making the change stick. Resistance is not a necessary outcome of change programs.

I have noticed that those responsible for introducing or implementing change in organizations frequently have a high personal need for chance. Often they are mismatched with their environment, and so, *do not speak the same language* as the people they wish to influence.

Why New Coke Didn't Make It

Once again, there is no substitute for good market research. Remember New Coke? Apparently, when they tested the taste of New Coke, the results were conclusive. New Coke tasted better than the old Coke. However, they could not have tested the *name*.

Let's examine, for a moment, the distribution of the patterns in this category. Only a maximum of 30% of the population in the work Context is interested in *new*, according to Rodger Bailey's work. But this was the soft drink Context. How many people do you think would want to drink something new in soft drinks, as opposed to what they know, trust and buy consistently? Apparently, not very many. Coca Cola responded and returned old Coke to the market. They called it Coke Classic, which is Sameness language.

Labatt Blue, a Canadian beer, apparently understood the pattern. They produced a billboard campaign with the slogan: "Tired of the same, old thing? Neither are we."

In 1992, the Saturn automobile was introduced. The commercials announced: "A different kind of company. A different kind of car." My ears picked up immediately. It would be interesting to find out what percentage of the new car market actually wants something completely different.

When your market has mainly a Sameness pattern, you will need to demonstrate how the product will give them something they know. It must look, sound and feel like old *reliable*. "You can always count on us" or "We'll always be there," like Roch Voisine's hit song. This can be a creative challenge for new products and services. How about: "Remember when you . . . It's back, just the same, and better than ever before."

Sameness with Exception customers want improvements. Show them how your product or service is better than the competition or what they had before. How it will make their lives easier (Toward), with fewer hassles (Away From). They will prefer to buy *upgrades* rather than different software packages.

Difference people want something totally new and different from everyone else. "You'll be the only one in your neighbourhood" (External) or "You can see for yourself how unique this is" (Internal).

If you want to capture everyone, you will need an updated version of *new* and *improved*, since that slogan is now old hat.

SUMMARY

DECISION FACTORS

Sameness: They like things to stay the same. They will provoke change only every 15 to 25 years.

Sameness with Exception:
They prefer situations to evolve over time. They want major change about every 5 to 7 years.

Difference: They want change to be constant and drastic. They will initiate change every 1 to 2 years.

Sameness with Exception and Difference:
They like both evolution and revolution. Major change averages every 3 to 4 years.

Distribution:

Sameness 5%
Sameness with Exception 65%
Difference 20%
Sameness with Exception and Difference 10%

INFLUENCING LANGUAGE

Sameness: The same as; as you already know; like before; identical

Sameness with Exception:
More; better; less; the same except; evolving; progress; gradual improvement; upgrade

Difference: New; totally different; completely changes; switch; shift; unique; one of a kind; brand new

Sameness with Exception and Difference:
Use *both* Sameness with Exception *and* Difference language

Using the Profiling Worksheet: Motivation Traits

On the following page you will find the Motivation Traits worksheet to help you master both asking the LAB Profile questions and recognizing the patterns of the person you are interviewing. A similar worksheet can be found at the end of the Working Traits section. The full profiling sheet (for both the Motivation and Working Traits) is included near the end of the book.

On the left side of the page are the questions to ask. I have emphasized the basic questions, while the work Context is in normal print. Remember that for LEVEL (Proactive and Reactive), there are no questions to ask. You simply listen for the patterns while the person is talking.

On the right hand side are the patterns and a summary of each of the clues for recognizing the patterns.

When I am interviewing someone I usually start off by putting one check mark each on Proactive and Reactive, since 60 to 65% of the population is right in the middle. Subsequently during the interview, if they use mostly one pattern or the other, you can add check marks in the appropriate place.

Often I will write down the expressions that indicate a particular pattern so that I can verify them when I review the results with the person.

Giving Feedback

When sharing the results of the LAB Profile with someone, avoid using jargon such as *Toward* or *Away From*. It will be more meaningful if you simply describe the behaviours of each pattern. For example: "You prefer to solve problems and do trouble-shooting rather than working towards goals. What triggers you into action is when there is a problem to be solved or prevented."

I have included a pattern summary in the Appendix to help you use layman's terminology when you are speaking to the uninitiated.

The LAB Worksheet: Motivation Traits

by Rodger Bailey

Name _____ Date _____

Context _____ Job Title _____

(makes things happen) (waits, analyzes)	**Level** __ **Proactive:** active, do it, short, crisp sentences __ **Reactive:** try, think about, could, wait
What do you want in your work?	Criteria (list here)
Why is that (criteria) **important?** (ask 3 times)	**Direction** __ **Toward:** attain, gain, achieve, get, include __ **Away From:** avoid, exclude, recognize problems
How do you know that you have done a good job in your work?	**Source** __ **Internal:** knows within self __ **External:** told by others, facts and figures
Why did you choose your current job?	**Reason** __ **Options:** criteria, choice, possibilities __ **Procedures:** story, how, no choice, necessity
What is the relationship between your work this year and last year?	**Decision Factors** __ **Sameness:** same, no change __ **Sameness with Exception:** more, better, comparisons __ **Difference and Sameness with Exception:** difference plus comparison

Part Three

Working Traits

Working Traits

The next eight categories of the LAB Profile will tell you how people deal with information; what type of tasks and environment they need to be most productive in a given Context, and how they get convinced about something.

These categories will demonstrate how to *maintain* someone's motivation.

Each pattern is described in its pure form.

At the end of the Working Traits section, you will find a summary Profiling worksheet to help you master asking the questions and recognizing the patterns.

The Forest for the Trees: Working Scope

> What size chunk of information does the person handle best? The big
> picture or specific details?

Using the Scope category, you can determine whether someone can handle
overviews and grand designs, or whether the details make more sense. There
are two patterns in this category:

Specific

Specific people handle small pieces of information well. At the extreme,
they cannot perceive or create an overview. They treat information in linear
sequences, step by step, in all its detail. A Specific person perceives the trees,
branches and twigs, rather than the forest. They may have difficulty
prioritizing as a result. If they are interrupted in the middle of a sequence,
they tend to either start over at the beginning, or resume the telling from the
point at which they were interrupted. Specific people work well where
details must be attended to, in tasks such as organizing events or handling
logistics.

> Note: There is a difference between a *sequence*, which Specific
> people use and a *procedure*, used by Procedures people. While
> both have a beginning and an end, there may be choice points,
> branches and several end points in a procedure. A sequence is
> chronological, linear, narrow and uni-directional. It is pos-
> sible for a person to *have both* Specific and Options patterns
> or a Procedures pattern in combination with a General
> pattern.

Sequence: A — B — C — D etc.

```
         _____C
      |        \ F __H
Procedure:  A — B     |
      |_____D____E_K___ L
            |____G
```

89

General

People with a General pattern in a given Context prefer to work on the *overview*, or at the *conceptual level*, though they can concentrate on details for finite periods of time. Because they see the *big picture* all at once, they may present ideas in a random order without stating the link between one thought and another. They concentrate on the forest, and having to deal with the trees for long periods of time irritates them.

DISTRIBUTION

(in the work Context, from Rodger Bailey)

Specific	Equally Specific & General	General
15%	25%	60%

Pattern Recognition

While there are no specific questions for this category, you will be able to recognize the patterns within virtually each sentence spoken.

Hint: One simple way you can know for sure is to time your LAB Profile interview. On average, a full interview takes about 20 minutes to complete, not including giving the person your feedback. With a Specific person, the interview will be at least 40 minutes.

Here's how to recognize these patterns in conversation:

Specific
- speak in sequences, step-by-step
- *lots* of modifiers, adverbs, adjectives
- proper nouns for people, places and things
- if they lose the sequence, they will start over again or continue from where they left off
- only seem to be aware of the step before and after the one they are on, not much perception of the overview

General

- may present things in random order
- overview, summaries
- concepts, abstracts
- simple sentences, few modifiers or details

Examples

Specific:
"Yesterday at 10 A.M. George and I met with Mr. Vivaldi, our big client from Rome, who spoke about renewing our shipping contract for the third year in a row. He now wants the price of the cardboard packaging to be included with the total price next year."

Mainly Specific:
"Yesterday at 10 A.M. George and I met with Mr. Vivaldi, our client from Rome, to discuss renewing our shipping contract. He wants to include the packaging in the total deal."

Equally Specific and General:
"Yesterday, Mr. Vivaldi told George and I that he wants to include the cardboard packaging in the price next year."

Mainly General:
"Next year Mr. Vivaldi wants to renegotiate our contract."

General:
"Rome wants to renegotiate."

Combinations

I am often asked that when someone is answering the Reason question from the Motivation Traits, how would one know if they were Specific or Procedures, if they are telling a story. The Reason question is: "Why did you choose your current work?" To distinguish between a Procedure pattern and a sequence, which is Specific, you will need to pay attention to the amount of detail given.

Here are some examples. The first one is a response from a Procedures person who is Mainly General. "I didn't really choose this kind of work. I was working in another company and they laid off a lot of people. I didn't have a job when this one came up. I applied and got it." Procedures, mainly General.

Here is an example of Procedures with Mainly Specific. "I was working for the Whoofed Cookies Beverage Company as a field engineer from 1973 to 1991. Then the company went into a period of financial difficulties, so in order to stop themselves from going under, they had to let 250 people go. They closed down my department and then I spent eight and a half months unemployed. I had made 30 applications in each of 3 geographical areas. Then Stephanie Slobdonovich from the Miracle Cure Cleaning Company called me, I had an interview the following day at 10 A.M. and was hired."

Here is what Specific and Options would sound like. "It was exactly the kind of thing I was looking for. I get to work with people. Different kinds of people. I get to work with tall people, short people, fat people, thin people. People with curly hair and people with thin hair and people with no hair on the top of their heads . . . etc." This is not a story, it is all Criteria (therefore Options) and described in what I would call excruciating detail. (If I have characterized that example as *excruciating*, what does that tell you about my own pattern?)

Here's another general hint:

As you become increasingly familiar with recognizing the patterns in everyday conversation, you will find yourself noticing and hearing many patterns at once, sometimes within a single sentence.

Influencing Language

Generally speaking, it is important to match person's pattern in exactly the way they talk to you when in conversation.

Specific

- exactly; precisely; specifically; details; use sequences and lots of qualifiers

General

- the big picture; the main idea; essentially; the important thing is; in general; concepts
- leave out the details and multiple qualifiers

When Bad Communication Happens to Good People

When a person with a General pattern is communicating, negotiating or problem solving with a Specific person, you may notice many misunderstandings. The Specific person may be concentrating on each separate example of a problem, for instance, and listing what happened in chronological order while the General person wants to get to the point. Where there is a huge difference in the size of pieces of information each is treating;

i.e. one is dealing with each item in great detail, while the other is trying to get at the big picture, several things will happen:

1. While the General person will be able to follow the specifics for a while, he will quickly get bored or feel drowned in detail and want to quit, leave or yell, depending on his preferences.

2. The Specific person will insist on giving even more details of information in an attempt to make things precise for the other person and will not understand the attempts of the General person to summarize the situation.

3. The General person may speak in such vague terms that she does not give enough information for others to understand what she is actually talking about. She may then lose credibility with the Specific person, who may suspect her of bad intentions.

So what is the cure? There are several options. (Wouldn't you know it?) First, you will need to realize that this is a situation which will take some time to resolve, because of one party's need for detail. This can be an advantage where the specifics of a contractual agreement need to be sorted out properly, and will save time later as they will not be overlooked. (You would have to have somewhat of a General and a Toward pattern to *overlook* something.)

You could ask a person who has both Specific and General to mediate between the two, essentially *translating* back and forth. If you are mediating, you will need to reassure both parties that their respective approaches are important and relevant, however different they may be.

For the Specific person, you will need to play back their issues and Criteria and then describe the sequence by which you will proceed, which includes translating items into General terms. For the General person, give them the big picture. "The main thing is making sure you both can understand each other; I'll help by facilitating that process."

Other alternatives include getting the Specific person to make a list of the important issues on one page in order to facilitate the General person's understanding. To help a General person be more clear to a Specific person, ask them sensory-specific questions such as "How would you know when it's right?", or "Can you give me a tangible example?", or "What specifically would have to happen?"

To capitalize on the strengths of each one, have the Specific person check the details of any agreement (especially if they are also Away From, so they can pick out errors and omissions). The General person will be able to determine whether the process is generally on track to achieving an agreement.

The key is making sure that each understand how they themselves and the other person are functioning. They can use these complimentary differences to mutual benefit, provided they accept them and adjust the process, as mentioned above, to take into account each person's needs and strengths.

When someone is highly Specific, how can you interact with them to help speed them through to the end of their sequence? One of the things you can do is ask them what happens at the end. This may be perceived as a sort of violation, but at least it is not an interruption.

Why Do All the Songs I Know End in la, la, la?

Here is an analogy to illustrate how someone who is Specific processes information. When people want to remember the words to a song, they usually start singing the song from the beginning, because the words are stored in their brain sequentially. So if you interrupt them, they lose their train of thought, and will have to go back to the beginning to pick it up again. Simply talking and responding will not make them go back, it is *being interrupted* that makes them start over. Asking them "then what happened?" may help them to get to the next item. By doing that, you are respecting the sequence and moving them on to the next step. The word "then" presupposes that something happened before, and something happened after. Another suggestion, if they are not an off the scale Specific, is to ask them to fast forward, almost as if they had recorded their thoughts on tape.

Hiring

Does the job require close attention to specific, sequential details for extended periods of time, or is detailed work of this kind only a small part of the overall responsibilities? Bookkeeping requires someone who can concentrate on specifics for long stretches at a time, while deciding financial strategies is much more an overview kind of task. People and project management tend to be Mainly General functions.

Many positions in manufacturing are Specific and sequential in nature, such as assembly-line work. General people would make many mistakes through inattention to detail in this kind of work. Quality control necessitates a Mainly Specific pattern as well as Procedures and Away From.

The essential question to answer when profiling a position is to *what extent is attention to detail necessary?* You would not want a pharmacist to generally get the dosage right when dispensing a prescription.

Difficult Bosses

If a manager is Equally Specific and General, she can be very difficult to work for. This kind of manager not only knows *what* needs to be done, but tends to become very specific in telling employees exactly *how* to do it. Because they, as managers, have a handle on both aspects of the work, they often will not delegate, believing it is easier to just do it themselves, or that they can do a better job themselves. When combined with a Co-operative pattern (please refer to Working Style), they do not leave any territory for their employees to deal with on their own.

Sales, Marketing and Submitting Bids

Prospective purchasers who have a General pattern will want broad descriptions that match their Criteria. As can be expected, Specific people want all the facts, listed in order. Print advertisements for technical products, or software often contain a lot of specifics right in the ad. These ads could be accompanied by another one for General purchasers, with a compelling image and a few words.

Many companies, when submitting a bid, do not know whether the purchasing group consists of mainly Specific or General people or both. Why take a chance on either giving too much information or not enough? Bids must contain a lot of detail. The *Executive Overview* will be read by the Generals, with an occasional peek in the Index to find the specific bits they need to complete the picture. The Specifics and people with a mixed pattern will need the full text to make their decision.

Life, the Universe and Everything

In Douglas Adams' famous science fiction novel, **The Hitchhikers Guide to the Galaxy**, the great question of life, the universe and everything was asked of the biggest computer ever built. After centuries of computation, and much speculation on the part of Galaxy philosophers, the wonderful computer submitted its answer to the waiting populations. The answer was: 42. Well, what can you expect when you address a General question to a Specific entity?

Pies in the Sky

One of the problems encountered by people who are "pie in the sky" General has to do with the consequences of staying in the conceptual realm. A friend of mine, who has a General and Reactive combination, had been the head of Human Resources for a large firm in France. He and the company went their separate ways because of some political disagreements.

I asked him, "What are you going to do next?" He responded: "It is important when one is to work with a company, that the policies and values be the same and what is really important to me is that we establish a humanistic philosophy." I said: "Okay. What are you going to do next to find that kind of company?" He continued: "It is important to understand that the philosophy must be right." I began to lose it: "So what are you going to **do** to find a job?" I shrieked. He needed to break the task of making his next career move into smaller steps and to have a plan of action for meeting his Criteria.

People who are very General may present things in random order (how's that for an oxymoron?), because they are looking at the big picture. They sometimes do not bother specifying the link between items or ideas, since they can see the whole relationship. Often people will not know what they are talking about.

We have discussed the two patterns. Do you get the picture? Or do I need to go into more detail?

SUMMARY

SCOPE

Specific: Deals with details and sequences. Cannot see the overview.

General: Prefers the overview, big picture. Can handle details for short periods.

Distribution: Specific 15%
  equally Specific and General 25%
  General 60%

INFLUENCING LANGUAGE

Specific: Exactly; precisely; specifically; gives lots of details

General: The big picture; essentially; the point is; in general

When Hinting Won't Work: Working Attention Direction

> Does the person naturally pay attention to the nonverbal behaviour of others, or to their own internal experience?

The Attention Direction category reveals whether a person can perceive, and respond *automatically* to the body language and voice tone of other people or not. There are two patterns:

Self

Self people do not show many emotions although they do have feelings. There is sometimes a time gap between when they receive a stimulus and when they respond to it. They respond based on what *they* consider to be appropriate. These people are convinced only by the *content* of what people say, rather than the accompanying tone, body language or level of rapport. They have difficulty establishing rapport because they do not notice other people's body language, and therefore they miss many clues. People with this pattern simply do not pick up hints.

They know how well the communication is going based on their own feelings. As a result, they tend not to be adept at interpersonal communication. At work, many Self people become technical experts in fields where communication skills are not essential.

Other

Other people have automatic, reflex reactions to people's behaviour. They are animated (for their culture) and respond to others with facial expressions, body movements and shifts in voice tone. They know how the communication is going based on the *responses* they *consciously or unconsciously* observe from the other person. These people are good at creating and maintaining rapport, provided they also have the other appropriate patterns.

DISTRIBUTION

(*in the work Context, from Rodger Bailey*)

Self	Other
7%	93%

One in Fourteen People

According to Rodger Bailey's research in the work Context, approximately, one in every 14 people you will meet will be mainly Self, if these statistics also hold true for the general population. From my experience, I believe that you will find more who are somewhere in the middle between the two patterns.

Pattern Recognition

There is no verbal test for this pattern as it shows up in body language or the absence thereof. To test for Attention Direction, I usually drop a pencil accidently on purpose. People with an Other pattern will spontaneously bend down and pick it up, provided they have seen it or heard it drop. Self people will not pick it up. When speaking to someone on the phone, I will sneeze or have a coughing fit in the middle of a sentence. Does the person say their cultural equivalent of Gezundheit or continue on as if nothing had happened?

The following clues will also be apparent throughout the conversation:

Self

- Absence of culturally appropriate behavioural responses such as head nodding, saying "uh-huh", etc.
- reacts only to the content of what you say
- doesn't "pick up the pencil"
- doesn't notice or respond to your voice tone
- little or no facial expression or voice variation

Other

- responds to both content and nonverbal aspects of the communication
- will nod head, move body, say "uh-huh", etc., as a response
- animated (for their culture)

Let's say I were speaking to someone who had a Self pattern and I, with my shoulders drooped, my bottom lip sticking out, and a whiny tone of voice, said: "I'm really happy to be here." She or he would think that I was really happy to be here. For this kind of person, unless you actually say: "I am annoyed and irritated," explicitly, they do not pick it up. Hinting will not work, nor will sarcasm as a method of communication.

While only 7% of the population at work are Self, probably many more are borderline; that is, having some of the Self pattern. You can recognize those people when you drop the pencil. They look at the pencil, they look at you, they look at the pencil and then they may eventually decide to pick it up. It is not spontaneous; not a reflex. A reflex action is something outside of voluntary control. Sometimes you can also recognize these borderline people because, although they may exhibit little nonverbal behaviour themselves (i.e.: facial expressions, gestures and voice variation), they may be able to notice and respond to the nonverbal behaviour of others.

Examples

There are no word examples for this category. Only behaviour observation will allow you to identify "Self" and "Other" patterns.

There is an example from American television. In a program called M.A.S.H., there was a character named Radar. He always knew what the other characters wanted or were feeling before they did. He was picking up signals and clues in a highly intuitive manner; an off the scale Other.

For a Self example, we can recall Pat Paulsen, a dead-pan comedian who ran for President of the United States more than once in the 1960's. He spoke in a completely toneless manner with a total absence of facial expression or gestures.

When I was leading one of a series of communication and conflict resolution seminars at the CERN (European Centre for Nuclear Research) in Geneva, there was an engineer who had a strong Self pattern. Much to the annoyance of other participants, he kept stopping the discussion to ask for more explicit definitions of terms. He was filtering for the *content* of what was being said. I asked the participants to do an exercise in groups where they were going to practise some confrontation techniques. One person was supposed to observe and give feedback while they each took turns role playing. When I went into his group, he was practically in tears because although he had understood that there was something to be observed, he just could not see or hear anything. I had to do some on-the-spot counselling to help him focus on what *was* possible for him to do.

The definition of a good host or hostess is knowing what your guests want before they become aware of it themselves. For example, when you are in someone's home and cannot find your salad fork, without you having to ask, does one of your hosts notice your dilemma and go get you one? A Self person would not have noticed that you needed one. You would have had to ask for it.

Communication

Some people have asked me if a Self person would feel uncomfortable in social situations? How does a person with a Self pattern usually know if the communication is going well? They will focus on what is being said, and how they themselves feel about it, without noticing the nuances of nonverbal communication and so may feel quite comfortable. An Other person can evaluate the communication by unconsciously picking up body language cues and listening to tone of voice. What is more likely, is that the Other people in communication with a Self person, might feel more uncomfortable because of the absence of the nonverbal responses by which they normally get feedback.

When communicating with an Other person, the quality of the rapport that you established is just as important to them as the substance of what you are communicating. Self people are not influenced by the level of rapport you have with them, so you will need to be absolutely rigorous in the presentation of your arguments or explanations.

Hiring

Self people usually do not succeed in work that requires the ability to create and maintain rapport. They are not suited for customer service work or dealing with angry customers. Self people do well where technical expertise is required.

In the 1980's while I was conducting a series of interpersonal communications courses in a large high tech company, I could often tell a participant was from the Information Services department, usually within the first five minutes of conversation. Many Self people became technical experts in information technology and other technical knowledge-based fields. They tend to do well there, except in situations where knowing how to play office politics is an asset.

Having made that generalization, I must say that I have since noticed many more Other people working in information services than a few years ago, as companies increasingly demand both technical and interpersonal skills. As many of you know first hand, electronic mail aficionados have even worked out ways to express feelings in text, by including voice tone and emotions in "emoticons" such as :-), (grin), ;-),(wink), :-(, (sad), :-Q (close but no cigar), etc. Using the UPPER CASE indicates SHOUTING. (My personal favourite is: *%-), which indicates that *I am having a bad hair day and I don't care.*)

Other people, provided they also have the Choice pattern from the Stress Response category, have the ability to empathize with others.

Once a Self, Always a Self?

In theory, the Self pattern can be either *uni-contextual* or *transcontextual*. Transcontextual means that the pattern exists across many Contexts for a person. Both are possible. In my experience to date, I have noticed more Self people who have this pattern across several Contexts than those who are Self in only one Context and not in another. One student told me about her husband, who "never seemed to notice what was going on." She felt she always had to *tell* him.

My advice would be, that it is more rigorous to test in different Contexts, rather than just assuming that someone who has a Self pattern will always have that pattern.

Influencing Language

Pay attention to both the level of rapport you have established and make sure that your propositions hold water logically. Remember Mr. Spock?

Self

- keep the communication focused on the content
- match their Criteria and Convincer Channel and Mode

Other

- they are influenced by the depth of rapport

There is no specific influencing language for Self people. Pay attention to your content because the relationship is not what they filter for. Be totally rigorous in what you say. Define your terms properly. If they are also Away From, they will cut your argument to pieces, if it does not completely hold water. There is no point in taking it personally, that is just how they function.

SUMMARY

ATTENTION DIRECTION

Self: Attends to own experience. Doesn't notice nonverbal behaviour or voice tone.

Other: Has automatic reflex responses to nonverbal behaviour.

Distribution: Self 7%
               Other 93%

INFLUENCING LANGUAGE

Self: Focus on the content, match their Criteria and Convincer Channel and Mode.

Other: They are influenced by the depth of rapport.

Freaked Out or Cool as a Cucumber: Working Stress Response

How does a person react to stress in the work *Context?*

Wouldn't you like to have a way to find out in *five minutes or less*, if someone can handle a high stress job?

The Stress Response category examines how you respond to the pressures, at work or elsewhere, that are *typical* for the Context you are in? This is not about how someone would respond to major life dramas, since almost everyone would have an emotional response in those situations. People respond to these "normal" pressures in the following three ways:

Feeling

People with a Feeling pattern have emotional responses to the *normal* levels of stress at work. They go into their emotions and *stay there*. High stress jobs can therefore be difficult for them to handle over the long term. To many other people, they seem to overreact to situations or be hyper-sensitive. They are well suited for artistic or creative work where emotion provides the juice. As salespeople, they find it difficult to handle rejection and may not, as a result, prospect for new customers as often as they should.

Choice

Choice people first have an emotional response to the normal stresses at work and then either return to an unemotional state or not as they desire, in a given situation. *They have choice.* Because they feel emotions themselves, they can empathize with others, or choose not to. They tend to perform well as people managers, as they can combine the personal side of the job and distance themselves when necessary.

Thinking

People with a Thinking pattern do not have emotional responses to the *normal* stressful situations for a given Context. They have trouble empathizing with others as they themselves do not go into emotional states. They will not panic in most emergencies, but keep a cool head. They are reliable performers in high stress jobs.

DISTRIBUTION

(in the work Context, from Rodger Bailey)

Feeling	Choice	Thinking
15%	70%	15%

Pattern Recognition

QUESTION: TELL ME ABOUT A *WORK SITUATION* THAT CAUSED YOU TROUBLE.

For Contexts other than work, simply substitute the Context for "work situation". i.e. Tell me about a buying decision that caused you trouble.

When you are asking this question, avoid having the person tell you about *all* the times they had a particular kind of problem. "Whenever a customer is unhappy with our service, I get nervous." Make sure the person picks one specific troublesome (not catastrophic) situation that he remembers. What you are to determine, as they review that situation, is if they go into an emotional state and get stuck there, have an emotional response and come out of it, or not have an emotional reaction at all.

Nonverbal Indicators

For the Stress Response category, there are no specific language patterns to listen for. To recognize the pattern you will need to observe and listen for nonverbal cues; changes in how the person behaves.

Feeling

- they visibly and vocally have an emotional response while describing a difficult situation
- changes in 3 or more of the following are indicators of a change in emotional state:

body posture, gestures

facial muscle tension

eyes drop

voice will change in timbre, tone, speed and volume

- will stay in their emotional state throughout their recital

Choice

- will go into their emotions initially and return at least once

Thinking

- will not go into their emotions

Warning:

It is possible when you ask this question, that the other person (if they have a Feeling pattern or if they chose to talk about a major catastrophe) may go into a highly negative or painful emotional state. For this reason, make sure that you ask the Stress Response question before the Style and Organization questions (Tell me about a working experience that was *your positive Criteria*. What did you like about it?) It is important to ensure that you do not leave someone in a negative state. Reminding them of situations associated with their positive Criteria will help shift them into a more positive frame of mind. If they seem to still be distressed, you may also have them change seats to help them get out of the negative state.

Examples

These patterns can only be recognized by observing and listening to those behaviour changes listed above, not in the language structure.

For a demonstration of the three patterns, please refer to my audio cassette series **Understanding and Triggering Motivation. The LAB Profile.**[1]

For a good example of the Choice pattern, watch Captain Kathryn Janeway (played by Kate Mulgrew) on **Star Trek: Voyager television series**.

Hiring

It is very useful to pay attention to this pattern because certain professions demand certain kinds of responses. For example, the Thinking pattern would be most appropriate for an airline pilot or an air traffic controller.

---

1. See the Resources section for details

Could you imagine what would happen if a high Feeling airline pilot were to notice another airplane aiming right for her plane? Air traffic controllers who I trained, told me that you usually can tell if the person beside you is having a *close incident*. The heat energy apparently *just pours out*.

If rapport and empathy are important in a job, then Choice is the best pattern to have. Choice people have feelings and can also come out of an emotional state, if appropriate, to look at the situation or take action. When you regularly experience emotions yourself, you can more easily recognize that other people also have feelings. If Harry stays on the analytical, thinking level as a response to Sally's feelings, he probably will not acknowledge the importance of Sally's feelings to her or even sympathize with them.

Many people in artistic careers have the Feeling pattern because art is often an expression of feelings and emotions. I discovered that the principle activity of the staff in many fine dining establishments (especially in Europe), is not customer service, but trying to keep the chef happy. Many chefs are highly emotional people. When they go over the edge about something, all hell breaks loose.

Incompetency Attacks

In sales positions, Feeling people often become demoralized when faced with rejection from prospective customers because they take it personally. It means that they would often feel stressed in that kind of function and may even be prone to what a friend of mine calls, *Incompetency Attacks*. An Incompetency Attack has nothing to do with one's real level of competence, which may be excellent. It is a strong, emotionally-based belief of incompetence, usually felt by someone with a Feeling pattern in that Context.

Career Counselling

When I am counselling someone about career choices, I pay close attention to this pattern because it gives an indication of how much stress the person can handle.

Passion

There are some other issues to consider. While a high Feeling person may be prone to suffering from stress, they also have a need for passion and intensity. When a person has both Feeling and Options patterns in a

Context, they are highly passionate about developing alternatives; a very creative combination.

Managing Stress and People

According to Rodger Bailey, most of the population at work have the Choice pattern (70%). This means that when faced with a difficult or troublesome situation, they will first have an emotional response. As a manager, you can assist by helping these people *disassociate* themselves from their feelings, if appropriate, by helping them change perspectives.

There are a couple of ways to do this. You can distort time by asking them: "Can you imagine what we'll think about this situation 2 years from now?" You can have them see it from someone else's viewpoint: "I don't think our customers will care much about this." Or you can have them view the whole thing from the outside: "If you were a fly on the wall when this happened what would you notice?"

For Feeling people you will probably have to hone up on your conflict resolution and mediation skills. To maintain their motivation, give them tasks that they can get passionate about. As they are working, watch for signs of distress and overload of tension. These people are the most likely to suffer from stress-related illnesses because they feel stressed more often than people with the other patterns. Feeling people may overreact, particularly in tense or conflictual circumstances. It would be useful for them to learn how to dissociate or cool off. (See B'Elanna Torres played by Roxann Biggs-Dawson, the half-human, half-Klingon in Star Trek: Voyager, for a clear example of a Feeling pattern.)

When faced with a highly intense reaction from an employee, create rapport by raising your tone to the same level as his while saying something positive or surprising. "I'm so upset about you being upset, that I am ready to tear my hair out!" Saying something like that will get their attention, so that you can then channel their energy onto a more productive path.

Thinking people are highly appreciated where there is need for someone with a cool head. These people spend much time already disassociated from their feelings and can be called on when a rational approach is needed. Do not expect them, however to create rapport with others who are in an emotional state, because they will have no sympathy. Thinking people, particularly if they have a combination with Internal, can however, take the heat and be able to stay in the kitchen!

Influencing Language

You can *rouse* people in an extraordinary way by simply *being there* and making *rational sense* of it all.

Feeling

- get them excited about something and focus on the emotion, using words such as:

  intense; exciting; mind boggling; extraordinary; etc.

Choice

- speak in terms that indicate you can go in and out of an emotional state:

  i.e. "You can get excited about this, and then realize that it makes good sense too."

Thinking

- present the *logical* facts:

  the cold reality; hard facts; clear thinking; statistics

Language Range and Culture

The use of highly emotional words is not necessarily an indicator of a Feeling pattern. Some cultures use superlatives as the usual way of speaking, while others avoid them as much as possible.

For example, I suspect that the use of superlatives is another difference between American and English Canadian cultures. You may have noticed that, in comparison to other English-speaking cultures, Americans tend to use vocabulary that hovers at the extremes; from the C*OMPLETE DISAS-TER*, on one end, to the *AMAZINGLY WONDERFUL*, on the other. The French and the Québécois also tend to do this.

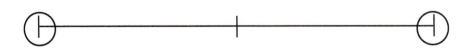

− complete disaster   amazingly wonderful +

English Canadians (and, in my experience, French Canadians from outside Québec) tend to linger closer to the middle, in a range that goes from the *PRETTY BAD* to the *PRETTY GOOD*.

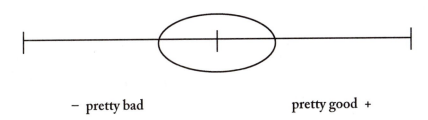

    − pretty bad   pretty good +

I've heard Americans talk about how difficult it is to get English Canadians excited about something. My advice to Canadians when listening to Americans describe something, is to apply the Monty Python rule of thumb and divide whatever they say by 10^2.

By comparison, the English, particularly the upper classes, seem to have an even smaller linguistic range; they go from *NOT GOOD*, on the negative side, to *NOT BAD*, on the positive side.

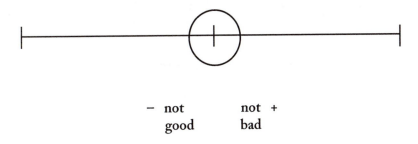

       − not   not +
         good   bad

To influence someone using the *Stress Response Influencing Language*, you will need to choose the kind of language appropriate to the culture.

---

2. This "dividing by 10" is from a skit in the British hit comedy television series: **Monty Python's Flying Circus**.

SUMMARY

STRESS RESPONSE

Feeling: Emotional responses to "normal" levels of stress. Stays in feelings.

Choice: Can move in and out of feelings voluntarily. Good at empathy.

Thinking: Do not go into feeling at normal levels of stress. Poor at showing empathy. Keep cool in high-stress work.

Distribution: Feelings 15%
Choice 70%
Thinking 15%

INFLUENCING LANGUAGE

Feeling: Intense; exciting; mind boggling; wonderful

Choice: Empathy; appropriate, makes good sense and feels right

Thinking: Clear thinking; logical; rational; cold reality; hard facts; statistics

I Wanna Do It *Myself*: Working Style

What kind of environment allows the person to be most productive: working alone, with others around, or sharing responsibility?

The Working Style category will allow you to discover, or confirm, how you can be at your best; whether you want to share your work with other people, do it yourself while involving others, or work all on your own.

In this category many people have more than one pattern; a dominant and a secondary Style in a given Context. There are three patterns:

Independent

People who have an Independent pattern in the work Context want to *work alone* and have *sole responsibility*. Their productivity suffers if others are around or if they have to share responsibility. When interrupted, they may lose their train of thought. They prefer to work in an office with the door closed. At the extreme, they may forget to consult with others (especially if they are also Internal). At work, they can go for long periods of time without craving contact with others.

The expression: "A camel is a horse designed by a committee," was probably authored by someone with this pattern. As a manager, an Independent person will do most of the work by himself and probably not establish rapport easily.

Proximity

Proximity people want a *clear territory of responsibility* but need to have *others involved* or around, in proximity. They need well-defined responsibilities, and to be productive and stay motivated, their tasks must involve other people. Their productivity will fall if others share responsibility and authority, or if they have to work totally alone.

Of the three patterns, this one is most suited for people and project management positions. They will make sure that everyone knows what they are responsible for. Proximity people do well as the boss, or when they have a boss, as long as territories are well-established.

Co-operative

Co-operative people want to work and *share responsibility with others*. They believe in the 2+2=5, the whole is greater than the sum of its parts, Synergy Principle. They have trouble with deadlines and finishing tasks if they have to work on their own. They do not need a territory to be in charge of, and as managers, will want to do everything *with* their employees.

The Californian light bulb joke describes these people. How many Californians does it take to change a light bulb? It takes six. One to change the light bulb, and five to *share the experience*.

Co-operative does not necessarily mean that the person co-operates, in the usual sense of the term, just that she needs to do an activity *with* someone else. When my oldest son, Jason, was about five years old, he spent an hour building a Lego boat. My youngest son, Sammy, then about two and a half, came down from his nap and kicked the boat to pieces. Jason was very upset, but from Sammy's point of view, Jason had *the nerve to do it all by himself*. He did not wait for Sammy to do it *with him*. This was intolerable for Sammy, who usually did not go off by himself and play. He may sometimes be disruptive when he plays, but he needs the company.

DISTRIBUTION

(*in the work Context, from Rodger Bailey*)

Independent	Proximity	Co-operative
20%	60%	20%

Pattern Recognition

QUESTIONS: TELL ME ABOUT A WORK EXPERIENCE THAT WAS (their Criteria)?

- their answer

WHAT DID YOU LIKE ABOUT IT?

For Contexts other than work, you can simply insert the Context into the question. i.e. "Tell me about an experience in a relationship that was . . ."

Make sure the person you are profiling picks a *specific example* of a situation that meets their Criteria. If they have numerous Criteria for the Context you are discussing, simply use one Criterion. Some people may never have had an experience that meets all of their Criteria.

For this category, you will need to listen carefully to what the person talks about. Listen to the answer for the first question and then ask the second question. Does the person talk about doing something *totally alone, in charge with others around* or *together with others?*

Independent

- says I, I did it, myself, my responsibility
- won't talk about or mention other people
- the activity presupposes that they did it on their own

Proximity

- other people are present but "I did it"
- may or may not mention others, but the *nature* of the activity necessitates the presence of others (i.e. sales or teaching)

Co-operative

- will say: we, us, our job, together, etc.
- includes other people and shares responsibility

Here is how to ask the above questions:

SRC:	Sara, what was one of your Criteria for work?
S:	Challenge.
SRC:	So can you tell me about a work situation that had challenge?
S:	It was a performance issue. There was a question whether a *particular group of people* were performing at the level they were supposed to. *I had to define who was responsible and what to do about it* because the performance wasn't adequate. *I* had to pool that together in different departments and the challenge was to come up with the solution.
SRC:	What did you like about that situation?
S:	I used creativity, it was stimulating, there was a challenge.

In the example that Sara chose to mention, we know that others were involved so it cannot be Independent. Sara says "I" and clearly demonstrates an awareness of who is responsible for what. Her pattern is Proximity.

In the 1970's, many of us learned how to say "we" and to "share our dilemmas." This is not necessarily an indicator of a Co-operative pattern. If it really is a Co-operative pattern, the person will talk about the fact that together "we" accomplished something, or that together "we" felt good. If the person indicates that this was his own responsibility, then it is the Choice pattern.

Examples

Independent:
> "I designed the new software and debugged it."

Independent and Proximity:
> "I designed the new software and then with my team I got all the bugs out."

Proximity:
> "I designed the new software with my team."

Proximity and Co-operative:
> "I designed the new software with my team and then together we ironed out the bugs."

Co-operative:
> "We designed the new software and debugged it. It was a great team effort."

Independent and Co-operative:
> "I designed the new software and then we all sat down and debugged the thing together."

Alternate Question:

How long can you work alone in your office without phoning or going to see someone?

Influencing Language
You can figure this out all by yourself, and use it with other people, so that you will all work well together.

Independent
- do it alone; by yourself; you alone; without interruption; you'll have total responsibility and control; just close your door and reroute your phone

Proximity
- you will be in charge; others will be involved but this is your baby; you will direct; lead; your responsibility is X and their's is Y

Co-operative
- us; we; together; all of us; team; group; share responsibility; do it together; you won't be alone in this (Away From); let's; we could do that

Team Players? Hiring and People Management

Many management and professional positions advertise for "team players", but what does this really mean? Most management positions require someone who can harness energy, orchestrate activities and create a vision for their team. These activities need a good dose of Proximity with only some Co-operative.

To understand what is needed in a position, you will need to look at the activities and the proportion of time spent in each one. Which ones are *do it aloners?* Which activities involve being responsible for the outcome with others involved, and which demand working together at the same time to accomplish the objectives? If the job requires a high degree of proficiency in all three, you are unlikely to find an ideal candidate and may need to redefine the position.

I had a job many years ago where I was the Assistant Human Resources Director in a national youth development organization for a region that included the provinces of Manitoba, Saskatchewan, and Alberta as well as the North West Territories. My boss had a mainly Co-operative pattern and I have Proximity and Independent patterns at work. She had us decide everything together and I just wanted my *own files*. I needed to have a territory, something that I could be in charge of. She was highly satisfied by our working relationship and I was frustrated.

People who have a mainly Independent pattern at work need space and time to themselves. They excel in those situations which call for someone to keep plugging away by themselves, even when all hell is breaking loose around them. They can concentrate for long periods by blocking out peripheral activities. They do not fare well where constant communication and creating consensus are an integral part of the job.

Since about 60% of the population at work is mainly Proximity, you will notice that most jobs have been designed to give people their own territory as well as necessitating interaction with others. Where the division of tasks has been master-minded by a Co-operative person, there is little mention of individual responsibility and this confuses and frustrates many employees. I suspect that the "open concept" design of offices was created by Co-operative types.

Where an Independent person has had a hand in job design, they may have left out defining how people will interface and communicate with each other. This leads to "the left hand doesn't know what the right hand is doing" situation between individuals and departments, common in many organizations.

Pattern Combinations

I am often asked if there are relationships between two or more patterns in the LAB Profile. Is there a relationship between Independent and Internal? These patterns do not necessarily go together. You could want to work all by yourself, not know if your work is good enough and have to ask: "Maureen, I've just finished this, can you tell me what you think about it." (Independent and External) Or, I could publish a report and decide that it was well done, without bothering to get any feedback. (Independent and Internal) Most of the patterns can go with any of the other patterns.

SUMMARY

STYLE

Independent: Likes to work alone with sole responsibility.

Proximity: Prefers to have own territory with others around.

Co-operative: Productive when sharing responsibility with others.

Distribution: Independent 20%
Proximity 50%
Co-operative 20%

INFLUENCING LANGUAGE

Independent: You get to do it by yourself; you alone; total responsibility

Proximity: You'll be in charge; with others around, you'll direct; lead

Co-operative: Us; we; all together; share responsibility; let's; do it together

Facts and Feelings: Working Organization

> How does a person organize their work? Do they concentrate more on thoughts and feelings, or on ideas, systems, tools and tasks.

Working Organization is about how people work, either by getting the job done or focusing on feelings. There are two patterns in this category:

Person

Individuals with a Person pattern pay attention to the feelings and thoughts of either themselves or others. Feelings take on such an importance that *they become the task itself.* They will organize their work so that they can focus on people and their feelings. They are good at establishing rapport.

Thing

Thing people concentrate on products, ideas, tools, tasks and systems (things). They treat people and ideas as objects, and believe that emotions have no place in the world of work. They want to *get things done*, and have a *task orientation.*

DISTRIBUTION

(in the work Context, from Rodger Bailey)

	Equally	
People	People and Thing	Thing
15%	30%	55%

Pattern Recognition

Since 55% of the population are mainly Thing-oriented at work, you will hear this pattern more commonly, although specific professions will have their own cultural pattern (i.e. many social workers have a Person pattern).

The questions are *the same as for the Style category*. In other words, when you ask the questions below, you will receive both the Style and Organization categories of information simultaneously.

QUESTION: TELL ME ABOUT A WORK EXPERIENCE THAT WAS (their Criteria)?

- listen to the answer

WHAT DID YOU LIKE ABOUT IT?

Person

- speak about people, emotions, feelings
- will name people, use personal pronouns
- people are the object of their sentences

Thing

- talk about processes, systems, tools, ideas, tasks, goals
- will not mention people often except as impersonal pronouns i.e. "they", or "you"
- people become objects, parts of a process

Examples

Person: "Mr. Richler was ecstatic with my report. I was quite happy with it too."

Mainly Person: "Mr. Richler was ecstatic with my report. I was happy too because it meant quite a breakthrough for the whole company."

Equally Person and Thing:
          "Mr. Richler was ecstatic with my report. It was quite a breakthrough for the company."

Mainly Thing: "My report meant quite a breakthrough for the company. My boss liked it too."

Thing: "My report meant quite a breakthrough for the company."

Other Questions

I recently discovered a test question which will allow to verify when you are not sure.

"Imagine that you are working very hard to finish a piece of *very important work* that *HAS* to be done in 30 minutes. A colleague, whom you *really like and respect*, walks in at that moment, appearing quite upset and wants to talk *right now* about a personal crisis. What do you do?"

Either the person will choose to complete the task (Thing), drop everything to comfort the person (Person) or waver between the two (Equally Person and Thing).

Alternately you could ask the person to "Tell me about a perfect day at work." The person will either tell you about tasks and things or people and feelings.

Here is another example of someone who is Equally Person and Thing:

SRC: Simon, what is it you liked about helping that person solve a problem?

S: The problem is fixed. And the person is important.

Simon is paying attention both with getting a solution and with the person.

When you ask someone to tell you about a work situation that met their Criteria and then ask them what they liked about it, they will usually reveal the element that has the most importance for them. The exception to this is when your interviewee knows the LAB Profile and therefore also knows what you are listening for. "Naive" subjects just give you their pattern.

Influencing Language

Just experiencing how great it is to use just the right words will help you achieve your goals.

Person
- use personal pronouns; people's names; feelings; thoughts; experiencing; this will feel good; for you; for others; the people; our team; our group

Thing
- use impersonal pronouns; things; systems; objects; tasks; objectives; process; get the job done; focus on the task at hand; the goal; the company

Good and Bad People?

Having a Person pattern is not an indication that you are either a "good" or a "bad" person. For example, if someone's profession consists of defrauding others, she would likely be totally focused on the emotions of other people. She will wind and weave emotions while spinning her web. Notice what Robert Redford and Paul Newman were doing in the film **The Sting**. This pattern simply describes *where* you put your attention.

In fine dining establishments, the maître d'hôtel treats all of the patrons basically like objects, placing them here while calling for service. But his job is to make sure that these *objects* are happy. The best example of that kind of Thing pattern for me, is on commercial airplanes. The flight attendants move down the aisle with the cart between them and you can see they are having a real conversation with each other. They're saying: "And you know what else I heard about him?" Then they plaster on a fake smile and bend down to one of the relatively immobile objects in a seat. "Would you care for a coffee?" You get your coffee and then they can return to their tête-à-tête.

Politicians also refer to people as objects. They talk about *the electorate*. What is the electorate? It is you and me, folks. But to them it is an object, a thing. When the Canadian population rejected the constitutional accords in 1992, many well-known national politicians explained the result by stating that "the electorate was cranky."

Hiring

At work, many jobs are organized to accomplish specific tasks and will need a mainly Thing employee. However, professional recruiters are increasingly looking for people who also care enough about feelings to communicate, establish rapport and solve conflicts.

Some jobs do require a mainly Person orientation. Customer service and reception are good examples of this. They also need to have an External pattern as their customers' feelings must come first. One of the secretaries with whom I worked had a strong Person pattern and was very fond of me. When I would ask her to do something, she frequently would drop everything and attend to me right away. I often had to tell her that it was not urgent and could be done the following week. She would also *not* do someone else's work right away, when she did not like them. In this case, she was also attending to their feelings.

Person sales people often will have a hard time asking for a close. They are having a lovely time communing with their prospective customers and do not want to end it by focusing on the task at hand. Person managers run meetings that get off topic for long stretches to discuss personal war stories. "That reminds me of the time ...." Thing managers do not recognize feelings and may hurt or embarrass others and then say "Feelings have no place at work."

Many people choose social work as a result of caring deeply about how people feel. Sometimes they forget that the task is to help people become independent and then move on to their next *case*. When they have a high Person pattern, they risk becoming overly preoccupied with the emotions of their clients and suffering from burn-out, (especially if they also have Away From and the Feeling Stress Response, which many do). For their own long-term well-being, these social workers need to create boundaries between themselves and their clients and to focus more on the task at hand (without neglecting their clients' feelings).

In the training field, a survey of corporate trainers was done in the late seventies. It was found at the time, that trainers tended not to worry whether they had achieved their objectives as long as everyone felt good. Today, trainers tend to be more task-oriented. Some people will say to me in a training seminar, "This material is very new for me. I don't feel comfortable." Since I tend to be more focused on the task at hand, my inside response usually goes like this: "So, are you being paid to feel comfortable?" However, as a professional, I usually respond by saying, "You know, discomfort is an interesting feeling, because it is a sign that you're stretching. And if you're doing something new that you're not used to, chances are you'll feel uncomfortable. Are you ok with that?" In my mind (with my mainly Thing pattern), making people feel at ease is a **means** to accomplishing the goal of learning.

Blake and Mouton noticed these two patterns when they discussed "Task" and "Maintenance" activities.[3]

Intimate Relationships

This pattern is also important in intimate relationships. Deborah Tannen[4] has noted that, in this Context, men seem to be more concerned with *reporting information* when communicating while women in relationships tend to communicate in order to establish and maintain *rapport*. She calls this **Report Talk** or **Rapport Talk**. These patterns are similar to Thing and

---

3. Blake, R.R. and Mouton, J.S., **The Managerial Grid** (Houston: Gulf Publishing Co., 1964).

4. Tannen, Deborah Phd., **You Just Don't Understand: Women and Men in Conversation** (New York: Ballantine Books, 1991).

Person. I would suggest that to communicate with a Thing partner (be they man or woman), you could establish rapport by giving or eliciting information. To get a Person partner focused on some thing, you would want to concentrate on their feelings first, much as I did with the 'uncomfortable' example.

Miscommunications between Thing and Person people can happen even over simple things. I was attending a course on Neuro-linguistic Programming in Paris and had lunch with a friend. As I was recounting a funny disaster that had occurred, Suzanne stopped me to ask: "But how did you feel?" "Alright, I guess," I replied and continued on with the next in the series of mishaps. She did not respond to the funny events, but rather: "But how did they *feel*?" she wanted to know. "I don't know how they felt," I said, starting to become annoyed, "but this is what they did." The two monologues continued. "That must have been difficult for you." "Yeah, I suppose, but what happened then was . . . "

At informal social gatherings, you can usually recognize the Person people. They are the ones who continue talking to you as you are trying to leave. Sometimes they are loathe to break rapport and end your visit.

Sales and Marketing

Person people will buy something for how it will make them feel. Hair colouring and other personal products and services are sold this way. "You're worth it."

To sell to Thing buyers, focus their attention on the product or service and the benefits.

SUMMARY

ORGANIZATION

Person: Concentrate on feelings and thoughts. They become *the task*.

Thing: Focus on tasks, systems, ideas, tools, things. Getting the job done is the most important thing.

Distribution: Person 15%
Equally Person and Thing 30%
Thing 55%

INFLUENCING LANGUAGE

Person: use people's names; personal pronouns; feelings; thoughts; feel good; people like

Thing: things; systems; the is; the goal is; process; task; impersonal pronouns

Why Middle Management Got the Squeeze When the Crunch Came: Working Rule Structure

> What are the rules for behaviour that a person applies to themselves and others?

Rule Structure will give you some information regarding the ability or willingness to manage oneself and others. There are four patterns in this category:

My/My: My Rules For Me / My Rules For You

My/My people have rules for themselves and for others. They are willing to communicate their rules to others. Because they believe that people are similar, they think that what is good for themselves will also suit other people. They will say things such as: "If I were you, I would . . . " A large majority of people at work have this pattern and probably in other Contexts as well.

My/.: My Rules For Me / I Don't Care

The My/(period) people have rules for themselves and do not care about others. They do not necessarily harbour malicious intent towards others; it is simply not their problem or concern. These people often get on with what they need to do without thinking about others. Sometimes they are called selfish by others because they simply did not consider anyone else.

I was often awakened in the middle of the night in my sixth floor Paris apartment, by people whom I believe had this pattern. They would honk loudly at 2 o'clock in the morning, in a residential district, surrounded by hundreds of people who had, presumably, been sleeping.

No/My: No Rules or Don't know Rules For Me / My Rules For You

No/My people do not know or do not have guidelines for themselves, but once given the rules, are quite willing to pass them on to others. As a result, they may have difficulty providing direction for themselves or making decisions. Instead, they may get stuck and not know what to do.

My/Your: My Rules For Me / Your Rules For You

People with a My/Your pattern know the rules and policies to follow at work but are reluctant or unable to communicate them to others. They operate from a "Different strokes for different folks" perspective. Because they believe everyone is different, they would consider it arrogant to tell others what to do. As a result, other people are often unclear as to their expectations.

These are the people who can understand both sides of an argument, as annoying as this may seem to those of us who take strong positions.

DISTRIBUTION			
(in the work Context, from Rodger Bailey)			
My/My	My/.	No/My	My/Your
75%	3%	7%	15%

Pattern Recognition

You will need to ask these two questions and notice whether the person answers both or one only, as follows:

QUESTIONS:

1. **WHAT IS A GOOD WAY FOR YOU TO INCREASE THE CHANCES FOR YOUR SUCCESS** (at work)?
   - listen for the answer

2. **WHAT IS A GOOD WAY FOR SOMEONE ELSE TO INCREASE THE CHANCES FOR THEIR SUCCESS** (at work)?

To identify these patterns, you will need to compare the answers to these questions. When someone does not know, they will hesitate a long time and respond with a questioning tone.

My/My:

- Same kind of answer to both questions or answers both questions easily.

My/.:

- Clear response to question one. Indicates lack of interest for question two.

No/My:

- Doesn't know the answer to question one. Has rules for question two.

My/Your:

- Has rules for question one. Doesn't know or wouldn't presume to say for question two.

Examples

My/My:	1.	Work harder. Be more organized.
	2.	Same way. Work harder. Be more organized.
My/.:	1.	Be more organized.
	2.	Not my problem.
No/My:	1.	Uhm, ah . . . Not sure.
	2.	Be organized.
My/Your:	1.	Work harder. Be more organized.
	2.	Everybody's different.

Influencing Language

If I were you, I would simply pay attention to what the person does because, after all, everyone is different, right?

While there are no specific words for this category, I have created some phrases to give you an idea how to match these thinking patterns in specific Contexts.

My/My:	"You would do that if you were him?"
My/.:	"You're sure about this and it doesn't matter for the others."
No/My:	"Now that you've been informed about what's expected, you can pass that along."

My/Your: "You know what you should do and you want to leave it up to the others to decide for themselves."

Hiring and People Management

People with the My/My pattern are well-suited for people management positions, provided they have the other requisite patterns; Proactive and Reactive, mainly Internal, mainly General, Other, Choice, etc., (and the knowledge and skill, of course). They clearly state what they expect of their staff and know and understand the rules by which they guide their own behaviour. If a job or a particular function demands that someone impart expertise, the My/My pattern is best. You would need to be able to tell others what to do.

In situations where a manager has an extreme My/My pattern, and particularly when combined with Internal, he can cause problems for the staff. In an organization for which I had done a large training program, the director decided that all the staff were to go through video-based training. His rationale was that this training had done him a world of good and would therefore accomplish the same thing for the staff. In my opinion, not everyone, at that level, was ready for that kind of experience.

When a manager has the My/Your pattern, she or he tends to create anxiety around them, because they do not *tell* others what they expect.

When it is important to discover the Criteria, values, goals, etc., of someone and then work with those, a My/Your pattern is useful. My/Your people make good mediators and negotiators because they can understand each party's views while maintaining their mediator's role. Much of today's standard training in listening and questioning skills for counsellors, coaches, facilitators, trainers and therapists aims to create a My/Your pattern.

Sales people who have a My/My pattern do well, provided they also have the other desirable patterns for their work, (Proactive, some External, mainly Procedures, Choice, Proximity, etc.), because they will ask for the sale. If they are extremely My/My, they may go overboard about telling others what to do. My/Your sales people may be reluctant to ask for the sale.

So, Why Did Middle Management Get the Squeeze?

The pattern often found in middle management in large, hierarchical organizations is No/My. These people do not typically set the rules for their staff, they find out what the rules are and pass them on.

Since the recessionary period of the early to mid 1990's, organizations have been going through many contortions; downsizing, "re-engineering" their processes, flattening the hierarchy, and in the process, pushing out middle-level managers, among others. Middle managers were perceived as adding little value to many processes, since they seemed to be merely policy and procedure *relay mechanisms.*

This function has been increasingly deemed unnecessary as electronic communication means become more sophisticated, times have been tougher financially in many sectors, and competition pressures have increased from around the world. The role that mid management plays as people facilitators has perhaps been undervalued, in my opinion, as companies were looking to cut heads.

As a result of this process of elimination, a large group of people with a No/My pattern suddenly found themselves looking for work, some for the first time in their lives. What can we predict about these people? It is difficult for them. They haven't got rules for themselves about finding a new career or a new job.

Many support groups have sprung into existence, specifically to help this group. They invite speakers to discuss job-finding strategies, raise one's self-confidence, etc.

Telling Yourself What To Do

I had a career counselling client with this pattern. I asked her, "Do you have trouble sometimes making decisions?" "Oh yes!, she said, "When they concern myself." I asked her to imagine that she was over there in another chair and then had her tell herself what to do. That solved a lot of problems for her. She had no problem telling other people what she expected but she had difficulty deciding what she expected from herself in the work Context.

My/. people do best where they can concentrate on the job to be done and not on others' needs. This kind of work is increasingly difficult to find as many companies insist that their people communicate and co-ordinate their activities. These people sometimes take a **"My way or the hiway"** approach and, if also Proactive and Internal, will bulldoze their way through whatever is going on around them.

I worked with the owner of a small environmental firm who had this combination. He had frightened most of his staff, to the extent that they were convinced a pink slip was waiting for them at the end of each day.

Switching Contexts

It is possible to have a My/My pattern at work and My/Your one in a relationship. Since My/Your people do not usually state what they expect from their partner in a marriage, for example, it may be useful for them to switch into My/My from time to time just to let the other person know what they want or do not want. Similarly, people who spend most of their time in a My/My mode in their marriage may want to shift into My/Your to learn how their partner perceives the situation.

I believe that by knowing the different patterns, you can start to choose which one would be the most appropriate at a given time.

Raising Kids

In the Context of raising children, do you also find out from your children what they want, understanding them to be who they are, as well telling them what you expect. In parenting, it is often appropriate to be in My/My mode. It is also fitting at other times to use My/Your, because one of the goals of parenting is to foster your children's growth and development.

SUMMARY

RULE STRUCTURE

My/My:	My rules for me. My rules for you. Able to tell others what they expect.
My/.:	My rules for me. I don't care about others.
No/My:	Don't know rules for me. My rules for you. Typical middle management pattern.
My/Your:	My rules for me. Your rules for you. Hesitant to tell others what to do.

Distribution: My/My 75%
My/. 3%
No/My 7%
My/Your 75%

INFLUENCING LANGUAGE

No specific phrases, just match the thinking processes in specific Contexts.

Decision Making: Convincer Channel

What type of information does a person need to gather in order to start the process of being convinced?

The information you will glean from the last two categories in the LAB Profile are especially important for sales people. The Convincer Channel category and the next one, the Convincer Mode, deal with how a person gets convinced about something. Until someone is convinced, they will not take the appropriate actions. At the moment they become truly convinced about something, they are most likely to buy the product or service, or to perform the task at hand.

For each given Context, people generally have a pattern about how they get convinced. There are two phases in this process. First people will *gather information in a specific sensory channel*, (Convincer Channel), and then they will *process that information in some way* (Convincer Mode).

Channel Patterns

See	They need to visually "see" a product, service or idea.
Hear	They need an oral presentation or to hear something.
Read	They need to read something.
Do	They have to do something.

DISTRIBUTION

(in the work Context, from Rodger Bailey)

See	Hear	Read	Do
55%	30%	3%	12%

Pattern Recognition

QUESTION: HOW DO YOU KNOW THAT SOMEONE ELSE IS GOOD AT THEIR WORK? (or How do you know that a car is worth buying?)

See	• have to see some evidence
Hear	• will listen or hear what someone will say
Read	• read reports, etc.
Do	• have to work with someone to know

Examples

See:	"Just by watching them."
Hear:	"When they explain their decisions you can judge their rationale and thinking process."
Read:	"I read their reports."
Do:	"I have to work with them to get a feel for how they work."

Sometimes people will have more than one answer to this question. For example, they may need to both *see* and *hear* evidence.

Applications

When you wish to convince someone about something, in a sales situation for example, or when assigning a task, you can simply match their Convincer Channel. If you know what kind (Channel) of information they need in that Context, simply give them the information in that form.

Examples

See:	"I would like to *show* you a sample."
Hear:	"*Sounds* alright, doesn't it? Is there anything else you need to *discuss*?"
Read:	"The *figures in the reports* are good."
Do:	"You'll want to *work with it* for a bit to decide."

Influencing Language

You can show a person what you are talking about between the lines, just the same way that they do it. Here is some sensory-based vocabulary for the above patterns:

See: see, look show, perspective, image, clear, clarify, light, dark, shiny, colourful, visualize, light up, vague, foggy, horizon, flash, get a look at, picture it, see it in action, view it, etc.

Hear: hear, talk, listen, wonder, say, question, ask, dialogue, ring, noise, rhythm, in tune, harmonious, musical, tone, discord, symphony, shout, discuss, hear about, tell yourself etc.

Do: feel, touch, grasp, gather, in contact with, connect, concrete, pressure, sensitive, solid, closed, open, soft, link, hot, cold, warm, try it out, make sense, work with it, grapple with it, try it on, test it out,etc.

SUMMARY

CONVINCER CHANNEL

See: Needs to see evidence.

Hear: Needs an oral presentation or to hear something.

Read: Needs to read something.

Do: Needs to do something with the evidence.

Distribution: See 55%
                 Hear 30%
                 Read 3%
                 Do 12%

INFLUENCING LANGUAGE
       Match the sensory channel (see, hear, read, do) with your language.

Clinching the Deal: Convincer Mode

> What does a person do with the information previously gathered in order to trigger a conviction?

After a person has gathered the information in a specific sensory Channel, they will need to treat it in some way in order to become *convinced* about it. This treatment is called the Convincer Mode.

There are four patterns:

Number of Examples

Number of Examples people need to have the data a certain number of times to be convinced, or to learn something.

Automatic

People with an Automatic pattern take a small amount of information and decide immediately based on what they imagine the rest to be. They jump to conclusions and once decided do not easily change their minds. They will often give the benefit of the doubt.

Consistent

Believe it or not, Consistent people are never completely convinced. Every day is a new day and they need to re-evaluate every time. I call this pattern the *Scarlet O'Hara* pattern because "Tomorrow is another day."

Period of Time

Period of Time people need to gather information for a certain duration before their conviction is triggered.

DISTRIBUTION

(*in the work Context, from Rodger Bailey*)

Number of Examples	Automatic	Consistent	Period of Time
52%	8%	15%	25%

Pattern Recognition

QUESTION: HOW MANY TIMES DO THEY HAVE TO DEMONSTRATE THIS (see, hear, read, do) BEFORE YOU ARE CONVINCED?

Number of examples
• will state a specific number of times

Automatic
• one example or assume people are good
• give the benefit of the doubt

Consistent
• never really convinced
• judge each time

Period of Time
• will talk about a duration or period of time they need

The question, as designed, asks for a specific number of times. People will either be able to answer that question or it will, at first, flummox them. Then you will know by process of elimination, that the pattern is *not* Number of Examples.

Examples

Number of examples:	"Two or three times."
Automatic:	"I can tell right away."
Consistent:	"You have to judge each piece of work."
Period of time:	"Over a couple of months."

Here are some sample dialogues, to show you how to test to make sure.

SRC:	Gillian, how do you know that an equal of yours is good at their job?
G:	I just need to see and hear them once.

SRC:	Once?
G:	Yeah, I can tell right away.

There's a hint here. Sometimes you will get the answer to both the Channel and Mode questions when you ask the first one. Gillian needs to see and hear, and has a Automatic Convincer Mode.

SRC:	Jim, how do you know someone else is good at their job?
J:	I'll see what they've accomplished and hear good things about them."
SRC:	How many times do you have to see, and hear that to be convinced that person has done a good job?
J:	Two or three times.
SRC:	(Let's test to be sure.) So if you saw and heard that twice, would you be totally convinced that they're good?
J:	Maybe.
SRC:	If you saw and heard that three times, would you be totally convinced?
J:	Yes. (Nodding his head)

Jim needs to see and hear, Number of examples: 3

SRC:	Natasha, how do you know someone else is good at their job?
N:	I would want to work with them for a while.
SRC:	How many times do you have to work with them?
N:	Uh, I don't know. How long?

Natasha's Channel is Do and she also revealed her Period of Time pattern while answering to the first question, confirming it in her second answer. Now we need to find out how long she needs to get convinced:

SRC:	How long would you have to work with someone to be convinced that they are good at their job?
N:	Oh, a couple of weeks.
SRC:	So if you worked with someone for a couple of weeks, you would be convinced?
N:	Yes.
SRC:	Adam, how do you know that a colleague of your is good at their job?
A:	I read their monthly reports.
SRC:	How many times would you have to read someone's monthly reports to be convinced that she or he is good?
A:	Well every report is different. You could do a good job on one and not on the next. You have to read each one.

Adam needs to read (Channel) and has a Consistent pattern for his Convincer Mode. He is never completely convinced once and for all; he judges each time.

Applications

Most of the population (52%) has a Number of Examples pattern (in the Context of Work), which means that they need to have the data a certain number of times to be convinced. Advertising often works on the theory that if you repeat a message six times within a given time period, most people will get the message and act upon it. Many personal development tape programs also recommend that you listen six times. The six repetitions will reach most people, because the majority need three or less to be convinced.

Consistent people take nothing for granted. Combined with Away From, this pattern is ideal in tasks that involve checking for mistakes or in any kind of quality control. You would not want Joe to think that since he 'knows' Charleen performs well, that he does not really need to check.

Learning

Let's take education as a Context for a moment. A child is learning addition or subtraction at school and she needs to repeat the sums 12 times to be convinced that she has learnt it. The chances are that she will never get the number of examples she needs during school hours, to convince herself that she can add or subtract. Lessons are usually designed with a certain number of repetitions of skill sets. If a teacher can detect how a student, who is having difficulty, gets convinced that they know how to add, then exercises can be adapted to provide the necessary repetition.

This information can also be useful for parents to help their children with school work. "How would you know that you can read well?" "When I can get all the words right away." (Channel: Do) "How many times would you have to get all the words right away, to be sure that you can read well?" "Ummm, lots of times." "Lots? If you could read all the words right away three times would you be sure?" "Hmm, I'm not sure." "Well, let's say you read all the words 5 times right away, would you be sure then?" "Yeah, of course." Then, as a parent, you can make sure that at each stage of reading, that the child counts the number of times up to five that they got the words. Once the child gets the *proof* they need, they will believe that they can do it and will read with more confidence.

You will sometimes need to discuss the proof with the child. If getting all the words or always getting the right answer is unrealistic, then maybe you could help them use a more attainable proof.

If a child is Consistent (never completely convinced) in the Context of learning, you will notice that he or she will need to get convinced that she or he knows something *each* time he or she does that activity. You might want to point out that this time is like *each other time*, in as much as, the child was able to do it, once again.

Tough Customers

Automatic people take a small amount of information and decide immediately based on what they extrapolate. In other words, they hallucinate the rest. Then they decide. They are the sort of people who jump to conclusions or make snap decisions. If you are trying to convince an Automatic person of something and they say no in the first breath, do not bother going back to try to reconvince them. They only rarely change their minds.

As customers, Consistent people are the most difficult to deal with. You will need to re-establish your credibility each time you serve them. They may love your service one day and hate it the next and love it again the following day. They appear sceptical and just will not get convinced. Use the same Influencing Language as for an Internal person, paying attention to match their Convincer Channel. "I suggest you try it out before you decide." (Do, Consistent) Or "Look it over and tell me what you think." (See, Consistent) This group is the most likely to return items that they have bought, or to change their minds on something they have agreed to in a negotiation.

Period of Time people need to have information over a set duration before they get convinced. Your customer may tell you that she needs to discuss (Hear) your product for a couple months. You can either respect that period or phone her a few weeks later and say that you have been so busy, it feels like a couple of months have gone by.

Influencing Language

Each time you are with people, you can give them the benefit of the doubt that they will consistently take the time they need to make up their minds.

(Remember to also match the Convincer Channel)

Number of Examples:	(Use the number)
Automatic:	You can assume; benefit of the doubt; decide fast; right now
Consistent:	try it; each time you use it; every time; consistent performance; don't take my word
Period of Time:	(match the period of time)

SUMMARY

CONVINCER MODE

Number of Examples:
            They need to have the data a given number of times to be convinced.

Automatic: They take a small amount of information and get convinced immediately. They hardly ever change their minds.

Consistent: They are never completely convinced. Every day is a new day and they need to get reconvinced.

Period of Time:
            They need to gather the information for a certain duration before their conviction is triggered.

Distribution:
            Number of Examples 52%
            Automatic 8%
            Consistent 15%
            Period of Time 25%

INFLUENCING LANGUAGE

Number of Examples:
            use their number

Automatic: assume; benefit of the doubt

Consistent: try it; each time you use it; daily; every time; use Internal Influencing Language

Period of Time:
            match the period of time

The LAB Profile Worksheet: Working Traits

On the following page is the second half of the worksheet to assist you in profiling someone's Working Traits. I have again included the indicators for each pattern to help you practise recognizing the patterns.

You can find a complete profiling sheet for both the Motivation Traits and the Working Traits in the Summaries section at the back of the book.

LAB Profile Worksheet: Working Traits

Name: _____Context: _____

(specific, concrete examples) (abstract or generalization)	**SCOPE** ___ **Specific:** details, sequences, exact ___ **General:** overview, big picture, random order
(attend to own experience) (attend to others' experiences)	**ATTENTION DIRECTION** ___ **Self:** flat, short monotone responses ___ **Other:** animated, expressive, automatic responses
Tell me about a work project that gave you trouble.	**STRESS RESPONSE** ___ **Feeling:** goes in and stays in feelings ___ **Choice:** goes in and out of feelings ___ **Thinking:** never goes in
Tell me about a work experience that was (use their criteria). What did you like about it?	**STYLE** ___ **Independent:** alone, I, sole responsibility ___ **Proximity:** in control, others around ___ **Co-operative:** we, team, share responsibility **ORGANIZATION** ___ **Person:** people, feelings, reactions ___ **Thing:** tools, ideas, process, systems
What is a good way for you to increase the chances for success in your work? **What is a good way for someone else to increase the chances of their success?**	**RULE STRUCTURE** ___ **My/My:** My rules for me/My rules for you ___ **My/.:** My rules for me/Who cares? ___ **No/My:** I don't know? My rules for you ___ **My/Your:** My rules for me/Don't know, to each his own
How do you know that someone else (a co-worker) is good at their work? (How do you recognize?	**CONVINCER CHANNEL** ___ **See:** observe, picture ___ **Hear:** listen, sound ___ **Read:** written reports ___ **Do:** do with, together
How many times do they have to demonstrate this **before you are convinced?**	**CONVINCER MODE** ___ **Number of Examples:** give number ___ **Automatic:** assumed, benefit of the doubt ___ **Consistent:** continually, never convinced ___ **Period of Time:** give time period

Copyright The Language and Behaviour Institute

Part Four

Applications

Applications

In this section, I have included examples of different applications of the LAB Profile. You will find lots of hints and subtleties on the uses of the questions, and on using the Influencing Language.

The topics covered in this section are:

- Career Counselling and Personal Profiles
- Corporate Culture Diagnosis and Change Measurement
- Hiring Employees Who Perform
- Building a High Performance Team
- Negotiating
- Analyzing Your Target Market
- Political Campaigns
- Education and Learning

Career Counselling and Personal Profiles

When people come to me for career counselling, we usually start by doing a LAB Profile. Also, managers have asked me to profile their employees to determine their strengths and weaknesses either for the job they are presently doing or possible promotion or transfer.

It is important to remember to clearly establish the Context in the person being profiled. Since most of the people interviewed do not know much about the LAB Profile, I usually include, in their report, the LAB Profile Summary, found near the end of this book.

Here are two examples of reports for career counselling:

LAB PROFILE REPORT
Bill X

Context: Work

Motivation Traits

The following patterns describe those things that will trigger Bill's motivation.

Mainly Reactive with some Proactive
Bill is more likely to think and consider than to jump into action. He is mostly motivated by situations where he gets to understand, analyze and think. He may wait for others to initiate and feel more comfortable responding.

Criteria
The following words and phrases are his hot buttons about work. He will be motivated when he thinks of or hears them:

personal and professional satisfaction, sense of purpose, sense of passion, sense of excitement, sense of accomplishment, part of something larger, provides a purpose for my life, sense that I am empowering people and organization

Mainly Away From
His motivation is usually triggered to move away from bad situations. He is primarily energized when there is a problem to be solved, a situation to be avoided, gotten rid of, or not have happen. He is a natural trouble

145

shooter. He will need to refocus on his goals at regular intervals to avoid being sidetracked.

Mainly External

In situations where he has to decide for himself, he can and will. He doesn't have a particular need to be the one who decides. His motivation is triggered when he gets feedback, either from other people or from results. In the absence of such feedback he will become demotivated. He may accept information as instructions.

Mainly Options

Bill is usually motivated to develop new options, alternatives, possibilities. He often has difficulty following procedures, but is usually good at developing procedures. When asked to simply follow a procedure, he may try to fix the procedure. Breaking the rules is irresistible to Bill.

Sameness with Exception and Difference

He likes his work situation to change often. When he is sure that he knows his job, he is happy doing that job for a couple of years. For some aspects of his work life he likes to do a job for 5 to 7 years, for other aspects he likes 1 to 2 years. His task clock seems to average at about 3 years.

Working Traits

The following patterns describe the work environment that Bill needs, the kind of tasks that suit him, his response to stress and how he gets convinced about something.

Mainly General

Bill usually makes sense of his work as an overview and prefers to work on the big picture, but he can work with detailed sequences for extended periods if necessary.

Other

He accepts the emotional content of his communications with others. He has automatic, reflex responses to the behaviour of people, which facilitates interpersonal communication. He makes sense of communication with others based on the nonverbal part of the communication.

Proximity with some Independent

Bill usually likes to work with others around and involved. To be most productive, he needs to have his own, clear territory of responsibility. For some aspects of his work, he wants to be totally alone, without interruption.

Thing with some Person

At work, Bill concentrates on the task at hand. While he recognizes the importance of feelings, given the choice, he will focus on the job to be done.

Stress Response—Choice with some Feeling

Bill initially reacts to job pressures emotionally, and may stay in emotional feelings longer than necessary. He is usually able to adapt to stressful situations and will respond based on his own belief of appropriateness. He is best suited to tasks where empathizing with others is an asset.

Rule Structure—My/My

Bill expects others to work the way he works. He has no difficulty telling others at work what he expects. He is well-suited to people management tasks because of this trait.

Convincer Channels—Seeing, Hearing and Feeling

He is primarily convinced about projects or ideas by seeing the evidence or observing the product or process. He is also convinced by hearing or discussing it. To be fully convinced, he also needs to "get a sense" of something, a feeling.

Convincer Mode—Number of Examples

Bill is convinced by 3 to 4 examples. This is the number of times he needs to see, hear and feel something to be convinced. Fewer than this number leaves him unconvinced.

Ideal Work Situation

The following points describe Bill's ideal work:

- time to reflect, analyze and understand with some time for initiating
- problem-solving and trouble-shooting
- feedback in terms of results or by significant others
- possibility to create options, design new procedures; less apt to follow procedures himself
- evolution and revolution; wide variety of tasks and major change about every 3 years
- prefers to work on overviews, rather than detail
- with own territory of responsibility, others around; some time totally alone
- concentrate on ideas, tasks, systems and some feelings
- avoid high-stress work

Suggestions

Bill needs to refocus on his goals at regular intervals. This will help him to assess his present activities as to whether they bring him closer to his goals and reflect his deeply-held values.

Since Bill has an aptitude to create alternatives and to reflect at an overview level, he will need to team up with someone who is more Proactive and more Procedures and detail-oriented to complete and finish the ideas he will develop. To succeed at an endeavour, he will need to divide what he has to do into steps and follow them.

High stress work with looming deadlines, for example, will not be healthy for him over the long term.

⸙

The checklist and suggestions at the end of the report can be used by the client when evaluating choices.

Depending on the profile of the client, you can either suggest options or give them a procedure for finding work, starting a new career, etc.

Here is another sample report for a client who was considering moving her part-time business to full-time:

LAB PROFILE REPORT
Claudia Y

Context: Work, present and future

Motivation Traits

The following patterns describe those things that will trigger and maintain Claudia's motivation.

Equally Proactive and Reactive

Claudia initiates or waits for others to initiate. She does either with equal ease. She can be energized while at the same time think and not act. Understanding is just as important as action. She is just as likely to consider as to act. She needs her work to provide the opportunity to do both.

To successfully set up and run her own business, Claudia will need to actively engage her Proactive part, particularly to generate new business.

Criteria

The following have a high level of importance for Claudia in her work. They are her *hot buttons*:

always have things to learn, work with words and language, contact with the outside world, team work, well paid.

The experiences represented by these words are what Claudia is looking for in her work.

Toward

Claudia is motivated to move "toward" her goals. She is motivated by goals. She wants to attain, achieve, get and is so goal-oriented that she may not recognize real or potential problems. She would benefit by having someone who has a facility for recognizing problems to help her when she is planning.

Mainly Internal with some External

Usually Claudia decides for herself and is motivated when she gets to decide. To a lesser extent she needs feedback from others to check how well she is doing, but generally Claudia knows within herself. She usually takes that information from others and evaluates it by her own standards. In her ideal work situation, she would have the opportunity to judge her work for herself, using feedback from others as input.

Mainly Options with some Procedures

Claudia is usually motivated to develop new options and to find other ways of doing things. She is very creative. She may have difficulty completing procedures because her main motivation is to develop alternatives. If Claudia runs her own business, it will be important for her to make sure that procedures are completed and that her ideas are taken to their logical conclusion before starting on a new project.

Sameness with Exception

She likes her work situation to progress and evolve. Claudia likes to do the same work for about 5 to 7 years. She can accept changes once a year, provided they are not too drastic. This is an excellent pattern for building a business, as Claudia will stick with the set up and development phases, provided she is doing activities she enjoys.

Working Traits

The following patterns describe the work environment that Claudia needs, the kind of tasks that suit her, her response to stress and how she gets convinced about something.

Mainly General and some Specific

Claudia prefers to think about her work in an overview. She can work with specific details for extended periods. As a manager or co-ordinator of other people's work, she must remember to let other people focus on the how while she manages the general overview. She can see the big picture at work and deal with details when she has to.

Other

Claudia is sensitive to the nonverbal behaviour of others such as voice tone, facial expression, body posture, etc. She has automatic, reflex responses to the behaviour of people. She makes sense of the communications with others based on the non-verbal part of the communication.

Stress Response—Feeling with some Choice

Claudia initially reacts to job pressures emotionally and tends to stay in emotional feelings longer than necessary. She is usually able to adapt to stressful situations and will respond based on her own belief of appropriateness. She is best suited to tasks where empathizing with others is an asset.

Proximity

Claudia likes to work with other people around. She likes to be the boss or to have a boss as long as her territory of responsibility and authority is clear. Her productivity will suffer if she has to work totally alone or if she has to share the responsibility with others.

Mainly Person with some Thing

While at work, Claudia focuses mainly on people's needs. This means she will be responsive to clients' and her boss' feelings. She can also be task-focused. At times she may drop the task to take care of someone's personal feelings. At these times, she may need to remember the goals and decide on priorities, which she has the ability to do.

Rule Structure—My rules for me / My rules for you

She expects others to work the way that she works. She understands the rules and unwritten policies of the workplace and she has no difficulty telling others what those rules are, an essential quality for management.

Convincer Channel—See and Hear

Claudia needs to hear and see evidence when getting convinced about something. To a lesser extent she needs to do something with the product or person to input the necessary data to start the process of being convinced.

Convincer Mode—Period of Time

Claudia needs to hear, see and do something consistently with the evidence for a period of 6 months before she is convinced. Less than this amount of time will leave her unconvinced.

Ideal Work Situation

In summary, Claudia needs the following elements in her work:

- opportunity to take the initiative and to reflect
- work towards goals (she needs to have elaborated specific goals or she will be demotivated)
- work that she can judge for herself with input from others
- opportunity to develop systems, procedures and ideas
- progression and personal growth in 5 to 7 year cycles
- concentrate on the big picture with a bit of detail work
- have the responsibility and authority with others involved
- rapport and empathy with others

Things to Consider When Deciding on Developing Your Business:

- be proactive about prospecting for clients
- have someone who can easily perceive potential and actual problems help during the planning stage. Explain their role clearly to them
- make sure that the procedures needed to make the business a success will be taken care of
- evaluate the business ideas and make sure that each plan is completed
- plan for incorporating growth and development in the work you do

&&

THE KEYS TO PERSONAL PROFILES

1. Decide on the Context and the purpose of the profile.

2. Adapt the questions to the Context.

3. Describe the patterns using layman's language for the patterns, when giving feedback to the person.

4. Make sure to include the ramifications of any relevant combinations, i.e. With Away From combined with Person, you can predict that your client will drop whatever he or she is doing to take care of other's needs.

5. Test your diagnosis by asking the alternate questions when you are not sure.

Corporate Culture Diagnosis and Change Measurement

There is a very simple, unscientific way to figure out the culture of an organization in LAB Profile terms. Ask the people who work there. In my experience, I have been surprised by the high degree of consensus among employees and managers about the profile of their company. While groups with whom I have conducted team building operations usually begin on agreeing about nothing, except that they have problems, they will instinctively know whether the organization is mainly Options or Procedures, Internal or External, Toward or Away From, Difference or Sameness with Exception, etc.

At the IBM International Education Centre in La Hulpe Belgium, the Managers of Management Development from each country did a Present State—Desired State analysis of the LAB Profile of the corporation. They affirmed that the company was Internal, trying to shift to External, from Procedures to adding Options, and from Sameness with Exception to adding some Difference. This analysis enabled these managers of education programs to understand exactly what kind of attitudes their programs should be encouraging. We then worked on some of the strategies they were using and could use to those ends. (But that is another book.)

To accomplish the analysis, I simply described the attributes of each pattern and asked the participants where they thought IBM was. The process took about three hours and was achieved by consensus.

You can also use the LAB Profile to measure the effectiveness of organizational change operations.

Do a *before* corporate culture diagnosis with a random group of people from the organization. Implement the desired changes with the appropriate strategies, paying attention to match your language to the Decision Factors patterns (Sameness, Difference, etc.) that are prevalent in the organization. About six months to a year after you have put the major changes in place, pick a different random group of employees. Have them describe the present culture using the LAB descriptions. The *effective* changes should show up by changes in the LAB patterns.

Hiring Employees Who Perform

An engineering and manufacturing company had advertised for a production manager. They received *300 applicants* and, out of that group, found *only one good candidate*. I was asked to profile the position and the senior management team to whom the successful candidate would report. I wrote their next ad with the appropriate Influencing Language, designed to attract the right people and turn off the ones who wouldn't fit. They received *100 applications* and *eight good candidates*.

Job Profiles

In order to profile a position, you will need certain information about the job itself, the environment and culture that the successful candidate will be working in.

For the position itself, you will need to understand what the specific *tasks* are and the *responsibilities* that the person will hold.

The following elements will help you determine the profile of a job. Does the job demand that the person:

- just go and do it / think about it / think and do (Proactive-Reactive)
- manage priorities, attain goals / identify and solve problems (Toward-Away From)
- decide by oneself, hold standards / adapt to feedback (Internal-External)
- follow procedures / design them (Procedures-Options)
- revolution, frequent change / evolution / maintain standards (Difference-Sameness with Exception-Sameness)
- big picture / detail (General-Specific)
- rapport with others (Other, Choice)
- high / medium / low stress (Stress Response: Feelings-Choice-Thinking)
- work alone / in charge of own territory with others around / together as a group (Independent-Proximity-Co-operative)
- focus on feelings / tasks to be accomplished (Person-Thing)

- communicate rules and own expectations / transmit received rules / just get it done / understand both sides (My/My - No/My - My.-My/Your)
- checking for errors, quality control (Consistent and Away From)

Here is the job description for the Production Manager mentioned above. This company designs and builds equipment for the manufacture of different kinds of plastic film:

PRODUCTION MANAGER
JOB DESCRIPTION

Manufacturing Production Management:

Manage plant workforce through supervisors.
Balance plant production levels with sales requirements.
Determine manpower and material requirements.
Carry out studies on unit (trade category) loading, capacity analysis and performance.
Monitor production reports and investigate causes of errors in production, shipping and data entry.
Release work orders to departments in accordance with master schedule.
Devise detailed production plans and schedule machine set-ups for trials and shipping.
Develop standard costing systems.

Ensure that shipments are properly done:

- completeness of order
- correctly crated/packaged/protected for shipment so that damage will not occur during shipment
- necessary assembly / electrical installation drawings are included
- shipping costs
- quality control

Interface with Engineering to establish priorities for jobs to be released.

Materials and Inventory Management:

Responsible for all WIP and stock.
Order and time deliveries from suppliers to co-ordinate with production requirements.

Maintain optimal inventory levels.

Co-ordinate and direct all activities relating to physical inventory audits.

Overlook bills of materials, determine production standards and part
  number.

Implement automated materials / inventory control system when this is
  feasible.

Co-ordinate / oversee purchasing department.

Negotiate prices / terms with major suppliers

Select / establish new suppliers

Bring new ways / methods to make the purchasing function more
  effective and to ensure that it changes to reflect the current
  environment.

Government Compliance:

Overall responsibility for compliance with applicable government regu
  lations with the plant. This would include:

- OHSA—Safety compliance and due diligence
- Workers' Compensation
- Hazardous waste removal
- WHMIS compliance
- Evaluations
- Discrimination

Facilities Maintenance:

Prepare annual budgets for supplies, spare parts and accessories.

Establish procedure for equipment selection, operation, maintenance,
  and replacement.

Using the above job description, and having profiled the senior management team to whom the Production Manager would report, I came up with
an ideal LAB Profile for this position. I have included it here to show how
I write job profiles.

PLANT MANAGER-JOB ANALYSIS

The following characteristics are to be preferred, based on the job description and the relationship with the Directors.

Motivation Traits

Mainly Proactive with some Reactive

The job requires a high level of energy and the ability to initiate, to a lessor extent the person must be able to analyse and reflect.

Mainly Away From with a little bit of Toward

The successful Plant Manager needs to be constantly trouble-shooting, inspecting for errors and making corrections. The directors will need to be goal-focused, with an eye on managing priorities.

Internal

The Plant Manager will have to set standards and evaluate against these standards. In order to fully assume the workload himself, he/she will need to know internally when things are good or bad and not have to rely on the constant feedback of the directors. To work well with the directors, they must agree on a set of standards and how they will be evaluated, and then let the Plant Manager get on with it.

Mainly Procedures with some Options

The Plant Manager will need to be motivated by following procedures most of the time. He/she must be the sort of person who is compelled to complete and finish what he/she has started. To a lesser extent he/she will have to develop new procedures.

Sameness with Exceptions and Difference

The Plant Manager will need to manage improvements and progression over time *and* be able to introduce new procedures and systems. He/she must also be able to handle a wide variety of tasks simultaneously.

Working Traits

Mainly General with a good dose of Specific

To work effectively the Plant Manager needs to always have a handle on the overview. This would allow him/her to delegate when appropriate. However, several of his/her tasks necessitate that he/she handle specific details for extended periods. Normally a person who is equally General and Specific has a difficult time delegating, which could lead to frustration on the part of his/her staff and burnout over the long term for the person him/herself.

For this reason, a person who is mainly General is preferable.

Other

The person must be responsive to tone of voice and body language to supervise and communicate with staff and negotiate with suppliers.

Stress Response—Choice

The Plant Manager will need to be able to empathize with others and be able to control his/her internal state. This will allow them to handle the work load without burning out when things go wrong.

Mainly Proximity with some Independent

Most of the tasks require someone who needs and understands the need for having a territory of responsibility while working with others around. For some of the tasks, he/she will need to work/think while completely alone.

Mainly Thing and Some Person

The person must remain focused on the task at hand and be responsive to feelings. Given ambitious production deadlines the task must take priority over feelings.

Rule Structure—My/My

He/she has to be able to give clear directions.

Convincer—Consistent

Ideally, a person who is "never completely convinced" is the best choice for a position which demands quality control and inspection. This means that he/she will constantly check and not assume that things are okay because they were last week.

MOST IMPORTANT PATTERNS

Upon analysis of the job description, and taking into consideration the Profile of the three Directors, the following patterns are the most important for the new Plant Manager:

Mainly Away From

Internal

Mainly Procedures

I used the following comparison chart to compare each of the short-listed candidates from the first advertisement (that the company wrote), relative to the 'ideal' for the job.

COMPARISON CHART

PROFILE PATTERNS	PLANT MANAGER	Bob	John	Mikhail
Proactive-Reactive	Mainly Proactive	Equally Proactive & Reactive	Mainly Proactive	Mainly Proactive
Toward-Away From	Mainly Away From	Mainly Toward	Away From	Mainly Toward
Internal-External	Internal	Mainly External	Internal	Mainly Internal
Options-Procedures	Mainly Procedures	Mainly Procedures	Equally Options & Procedures	Mainly Options
Sameness & Difference	Sameness w/ Exceptions & some Difference	Sameness & Difference	Sameness w/ Exceptions	Difference & some Sameness w/ Exceptions
Specific-General	Mainly General & some Specific	Mainly General	Mainly General	Mainly General
Self-Other	Other	Other	Other	Self & Other
Independent-Proximity-Cooperative	Mainly Proximity, some Independent	Coop with some proximity	Proximity	Mainly Proximity with some Cooperative
Person-Thing	Mainly Thing & some Person	Equally person & Thing	Mainly Person & some Thing	Mainly Thing
Stress Response	Choice	Choice	Choice	Choice
Rule Structure	My/My	My/Your	My/Your with some My/My	MY/My
Convincer	Ideally, Consistent	Consistent	Period of Time	Large Number of examples, possibly Consistent

RECOMMENDATIONS

In my opinion, regarding the attributes of each candidate (not the skills or knowledge base), John is the most suitable, followed by Bob. I believe that John is the best because of his ability to perceive, predict, prevent and solve problems and because of his proficiency at making decisions. He is the most likely to relieve the Directors of many responsibilities.

Bob is more goal-oriented and may tend to overlook problems. Because he is more External, he is more likely to need feedback on a continuing basis to help him decide.

Attracting Only the Right People: Career Advertisements

To demonstrate how to write an advertisement, here are the two ads used for the Production Manager position.

The ad placed by the company before I was asked to profile the position:

PLANT MANAGER

Private fast growing engineering company manufacturing high tech quality machinery for world wide export has immediate opening for decision maker to manage production division.

Production to double within the next year necessitates efficient co-ordination of rapidly expanding department.

Right candidate must have minimum 10 years related experience. Emphasis on organization, planning and purchasing. Candidates must have excellent people management and leadership skills.

Here is the ad I wrote after doing the profiles:

PLANT MANAGER

Immediate opening for a proactive Plant Manager who will grow with this engineering company, which manufactures high tech quality machinery for world wide export.

The right candidate will manage the production division, solving technical, people and government compliance issues by following procedures and developing new ones when necessary. You will set standards and assure they are consistently met, even under the pressure of ambitious delivery targets. You are highly experienced and skilled in project and people management and purchasing, and can prove it.

The first step is to call now for all the information you need.

I suggested that the candidates call because only Proactive people will actually pick up the phone. Can you identify the specific Influencing Language used in the second ad?

Building a High-Performance Team

As a people manager, it is incumbent upon you to accurately assess the strengths of your people. Beyond being aware of their knowledge and skill levels, when you also know their LAB Profile, you are better placed to redesign or adapt individual task assignments (where you are able to do this).

One way of doing this is to list all the activities that must be done in your department, and verifying that each one is indeed necessary and useful. (Many companies are now doing such task analysis with consultants in business process re-engineering to determine just what tasks are needed given increased customer expectations.) Using the elements from the Job Profile section, you can list the ideal LAB Profile patterns beside each activity, along with the knowledge and skill requirements.

Once you have profiled and given feedback to each of your staff members, you can adjust task assignment based on what needs to be done and the profile of your staff. I suggest that you do this in a consultative manner, taking into account preferences where feasible.

Let's look at the team as a whole. What are the elements in LAB Profile terms that characterize your team? What are the strengths and weaknesses when you consider the tasks that need to be accomplished? How can you maximize these strengths? How can you attenuate, or take advantage, of the weaknesses when pursuing team goals and objectives?

This is an area where there is no one miracle recipe. Your team will first need to decide its vision, mission and goals (within the larger Context, of course). There are many books on the numerous available methods for doing this. The next step is to assess your resources (including your people) and to evaluate where you are now in terms of performance. Any intervention you decide upon will then come as a result of comparing:

1. Your desired state and your resources, with

2. Your present state

I would like to give you an example where I used the LAB Profile to help a team improve its performance. I assisted the department of Pharmaceutical Services at a leading edge university hospital. After they had clarified, in both general and specific terms, where they were going, I profiled the entire team and the tasks to be accomplished.

Here is a comparison chart of what I found when comparing three Contexts: the *overall* work of the pharmacists, work in the *dispensary* and the *clinical* work they do on the wards, with the group profile.

PHARMACIST LAB PROFILE

OVERALL JOB	DISPENSARY WORK	CLINICAL WORK	PHARMACISTS n= 17
Proactive & Reactive	Mainly Reactive	Proactive & Reactive	Proactive & Reactive
Mainly Away From, some Toward	Away From	Away From	Mainly Away From
Mainly Internal	Internal	Internal & External	evenly distributed between Internal & External
Procedures to Options (2 to 1)	Mostly Procedures	Options & Procedures	Mainly Options
Sameness w/ except & some Difference	Sameness with Exception	Sameness w/ Exception	Mainly Sameness w/ Except, some with double pattern
Mainly Specific	Mainly Specific	Mainly Specific & some General	Mainly General
Other	Other	Other	Other
Proximity	Proximity	Proximity	Mainly Proximity
Thing with some Person	Thing	Person & Thing	evenly distributed Person, Thing & both
Choice	Choice or Thinking	Choice	Mainly Choice
My/My	My/My	Mainly My/My & some My/Your	My/My

While it is obvious that there are strengths where the group profile matches the job to be done and possible weaknesses where the patterns do not match, there are also other performance factors to consider. This particular group holds frequent departmental meetings to discuss work with patients, how to introduce and manage new technological developments and how to move the department towards its goals in improvement of quality.

Given that the group is mainly Away From, with about one-half highly Internal and mainly Options, I was able to predict what their meetings were like. A problem would be raised, solutions suggested and then long-winded disagreements would ensue on what was wrong with the analysis and suggested solutions. Many members of the team were frustrated by the length, frequency and lack of productiveness of these meetings.

We discussed ways to create more effective meetings by taking advantage of the strengths in the team. For example, they would need to discuss and agree on Criteria and standards to be met (Internal). "What do we want instead of the current situation?" They also specified what tangible evidence would demonstrate that standards had been met by asking: "How would we know we had achieved what we wanted?" Then they could explore options for how to get there. The Away From people would have free rein to examine the suggested solutions for problems and fix them. Lastly the few Procedures people on this team could ensure that the resulting tasks would be completed.

Interestingly enough for this group, given that the profile of their job had a good dose of following Procedures, most of the group fell on the Options side of that continuum. This may be an example that illustrates how one needs to take into account the culture of the organization. This hospital is a teaching and research hospital, known for its innovations in health care. Perhaps the institution itself attracts Options people to work there because of its reputation. I questioned the pharmacists about how they view their job. Do they see their day to day work as basically following procedures? Many of them said that each patient is different, with a problem that needs to be solved, as they search for *new options* with their multi-disciplinary team of doctors, nurses, etc. I would like to be able to profile Pharmacists in other institutions to see if this group is actually different.

They recently hired a more Procedures manager to balance the team. She has contributed greatly by establishing more protocols and ensuring that they are followed. I continue to help them with hiring new staff.

While it is difficult to make generalizations about how to create a high performance team, I believe that a thorough knowledge of your team members and the jobs to be done are the starting points. You will need to reflect upon the individual attributes of your team members in comparison to the mission, tasks and specific goals. (Am I My/My or what?)

Using the LAB Profile to do employee and group profiles, and comparing the profiles to the tasks that need to be done will enable you to identify areas that need improvement and areas where your team can go from good to great. You will need to have some Options thinking about this, because no one step-by-step process will fit all cases.

Negotiating and Bargaining

While the LAB Profile itself is not a protocol for negotiating, it can be effectively used for understanding the needs and communication style of all parties. It will allow you to present your case in ways that your partners in negotiation can best accept what you are proposing.

At the risk of making a gross generalization, certain groups or sectors have identifiable cultures that can be understood in LAB Profile terms. For example, a combination found frequently in union bargaining units is the following: Reactive, Away From, Internal, Procedures, Sameness and Consistent. People with this combination will react to management initiatives by noticing what is wrong (from their perspective) with any proposal, will decide based on their own standards and Criteria, insist on following the same procedures to the letter and will protest loudly when conditions and demands change.

They tend to ask for identical treatment of workers (Sameness) and therefore will fight the introduction of systems such as merit pay (Difference). *Fairness* is a word one hears often in this Context. It is a Sameness word. *Fair* usually means the same treatment for everyone.

As a result, to effectively negotiate with a partner having the above combination, I would recommend that you give your rationale in terms of the problems for the workers that would be prevented or solved. As they are probably Internal, you could ask them to *consider* the disastrous alternatives. Forget about suggesting options. "The *right way*, to avoid treating anyone *unfairly* would be to . . . "

Remember, that if you are negotiating with people who have a Consistent pattern, you will need to re-establish rapport and credibility at each contact, whether in person, on the phone or in writing. I put the Consistent pattern in perspective for a newly-hired general manager. He was taking his company through a turn-around, starting in a situation with historically bad labour-management relations. "In order to convince your workforce that you want to make the company and the workers thrive," I told him, "You will have to prove your good faith many times. You will only need to screw up *once*, in their eyes, to destroy all the goodwill you have been creating." (Consistent)

For union negotiators, I would suggest that your proposals be put in Toward and Internal terms, listing the concrete benefits for them to consider. Management tends to understand and agree more readily to forward-moving, goal-oriented proposals.

Preparation is the Key

To get ready for a negotiation, spend some time analyzing your counter-parts in LAB Profile terms. In cases where you have yet to meet, and cannot pre-establish contact by phone, look at any written communication you have received from them for phrases that resemble the Influencing Language patterns.

Alternatively, you could plan to ask some of the LAB questions in your first meeting, such as "Why is that important?", or "How will you know when this negotiation is successful?", etc.

When I am negotiating, I usually assume that the person I am negotiating with is Internal in that Context, unless there is proof to the contrary. This allows me to avoid being perceived as disrespectful and creates a climate where both our views will be honoured.

Sometimes you will find that a person is Internal in the Context of the negotiation and External to her or his perceived constituency. In this case you will need to use both sets of Influencing Language, while being careful to place each in the correct Context. "Only you can judge if your constituents will approve this," or "Having studied this to the depth you have, when you decide on the right answer, your people will show their appreciation for all the work you've done," or "What do *you* think about the impact this will have?"

The key to using the LAB Profile in negotiating situations is to take the necessary preparation time to figure out what your counter-parts' (and your clients', if you are representing them) main patterns are. This will guide you in how to present or discuss issues with them.

Hitting the Target:
Analyzing Your Market

Rodger Bailey, the developer of the LAB Profile, and I did some consulting for a major software company. They wanted to have a profile of their print advertisements (both media and flyers) to find out who they were reaching and to test consistency within the advertisements. Specifically, we looked at two elements; the overall visual aspect (that which would first attract a person to look at the ad), and secondly what was contained in the content (mainly text) of the ad.

We examined the ads and found that nine of the fourteen categories were represented. We analyzed the findings using a macro written by Rodger for a spread sheet program. Here is a summary of our findings.

Level (Proactive—Reactive): The ads matched the normal pattern for the general population at work.

Direction (Toward— Away From): The ads were skewed in the Toward direction.

Source (Internal—External): The ads focused mainly on attracting an Internal audience, although this pattern was not as clear as some of the others.

Reason (Options—Procedures): The ads represented both Options and Procedures.

Decision Factors (Sameness, Sameness with Exception, Both, Difference): While the ads generally showed a normal distribution (mainly Sameness with Exception)[1], the visual aspects of the ads were much more Difference than the body text. This means that people with a high Difference pattern would be attracted to the ad and then *not* find what they were looking for in the content.

Scope (General—Specific): While a normal distribution is skewed towards General, the ads contained much more Specific data. Our client and ourselves felt that this matched the corporate buyer of software fairly closely.

---

1. based on Rodger Bailey's findings

Style (Independent—Proximity—Co-operative): The ads reflected heavy clusters around Proximity and Independent. We suggested that it would be useful to determine if our client's marketplace is actually shaped that way.

Organization (Person—Thing): The ads contained a strong Thing orientation, which was probably appropriate for the Context.

Convincer Channel (See, Hear, Read, Do): For the flyers, the visual aspects used mainly Do, while the text was mainly See and Read. Once again, what attracted the reader was not to be found in the content.

As a result of this analysis, our client was able to determine whether their ads and flyers were reaching their desired audience for the two products that we profiled. By using data collected from their 800 information telephone line, it gave them the ability to test whether people with certain patterns were or were not responding to the ads.

We also demonstrated a startling fact for our client. I put the ads into two piles stating that one group had been written by one person and that the other group was written by someone else. This was verified by the account executive of their advertising company. We had clearly demonstrated that the writing was more influenced by the writer's profile than by the ability to reach a certain audience.

We would have liked to do more work with them to help specify the ideal Influencing Language for each of the products, based on re-interpreting market research already done, into LAB profile terms. Unfortunately for us, our client, was himself a high Options and Difference person. Before we could get to the next step, he had left the marketing director position and had moved on within the company. He now works for a competitor, in a different city. Plus ça change . . .

Market Research

Surveying your marketplace can be done simply and inexpensively using the LAB Profile. You can do it by phoning your sample group. You will need to adapt your questions for the appropriate Context, i.e.: toothpaste, using rail service, buying a car, etc. You may well find, after profiling, that only a few of the categories are relevant for your product or service. You can then design your advertising or sales procedure around the Influencing Language for the people most likely to buy.

Alternatively, if your product meets the needs of groups you are not presently reaching, you can switch some of your language and images.

You can also use the LAB Profile to re-interpret research that you have already completed. For one of the products in the software example, the *innovators* and *early adopters* segments of the market match the Difference pattern in the LAB. *Mid and late adopters* together, have generally the same distribution and behaviours as Sameness with Exception people.

The advantage of translating your research into LAB terms is to determine exactly what *Influencing Language* will be the most effective in your marketing campaign and sales literature.

Sales, Sales and More Sales

There are two main keys to producing extraordinary sales results by using the LAB Profile.

You will first need to adapt the LAB questions for your particular product or service. I suggest that you go through the list of questions and add in your particular Context, as follows.

"What do you want in a house?" or "What is important to you when you purchase software?" (Criteria)

"Why is reliability (their Criterion) important for you right now?" (Toward-Away From)

"How would you know if you did a good job at buying the right car?" (Internal-External)

"Why did you choose your last life insurance broker?" (Options-Procedures)

"What is the relationship between the place you live in now and your last one?" (Sameness-Difference, etc.)

"How do you know that a stereo is worth buying?" (Convincer Channel)

"How many times would you have to (see, hear, do, read) that to be convinced it's for you?" (Convincer Mode)

As you adapt the questions you will notice that certain of the patterns are more relevant to your product or service than others. In my experience, I find that paying attention to the Motivation Traits and the Convincer Channel and Mode are sufficient in most sales situations. Also your product or service may naturally attract people with particular patterns in that Context. For example, rust paint is usually sold to avoid or fix rust problems.

When you are in the process of finding out what your prospective customer needs you build in the adapted questions to your normal conversational procedure. You will then know how to present your product or service, by matching their Criteria and using the appropriate Influencing Language.

By following this simple process you can dramatically shorten your sales cycle and increase customer satisfaction at the same time.

Who Can Sell and Who Can't?

Those of you attracted to multi-level marketing (MLM) businesses and other sales careers *solely* because of "unlimited income possibilities" (Options) need to realize that your chances for success are, in fact, limited. Those of you who would do almost anything rather than pick up the phone and speak to someone you don't know (Reactive), need either to overcome this obstacle or consider going into retail sales, because most of the time customers do not come to you delivered on a silver platter. This is your career, and it is in your own best interest to find one with tasks that suit you.

Most sales activities consist of *following a procedure*. For you to succeed in sales over the long term, you will need to be able to follow a procedure over and over again. This means having a mainly Procedures pattern in the Context of your work. For outside sales and generating new business you will also need to be in a very Proactive mode, to go out and prospect for new business.

Sales is a wonderful career for those of us who like to go out and take people through the process of finding what they really need and want. When you systematically use the tools in **Words That Change Minds** to help you satisfy your customers' desires, you will find that the results astonish you.

Political Campaigns

Political campaigns provide the most dynamic example of the LAB Profile in action. The 1993 Canadian federal election is a case in point: the winning Liberal party used language that precisely matched the mood and aspirations of the voting public.

The polls indicated that voters were very cynical about politicians, their campaign promises and likely behaviour once elected. In LAB Profile terms we can interpret this as an Away From and Internal combination. The theme of the governing Conservatives was: We are *different*, relying on the pre-election popularity of their *new* leader, Kim Campbell. Wrong pattern. With the prevailing mood of cynicism, no one believed them. (Remember George Bush's famous pronouncement: "Read my lips. No new taxes.")

The Liberals produced their Red Book, with their commitments for after the election. Instead of telling people what to do (which would only work for people who are External), they told the public 'we understand you are *fed up* with campaign rhetoric.' (Away From) They presented their program from the Red Book and asked voters to *decide for themselves*. (Internal) They also proposed that since they had put it all in writing, the electorate could *judge their performance* (Internal) once in power by verifying whether they had kept their commitments.

But the Liberal party went further than matching voter cynicism. They redirected the electorate by creating hope, with their positive visions for the future of the country. Contrast this with Kim Campbell's flat declaration that there would be no upswing in employment until the year 2000. Which party would you rather vote for?

The Conservative party not only lost its large majority but returned *only two* Members of Parliament to the House of Commons. (This makes the Conservatives the only party in the history of Canada to have achieved gender parity.)

The Notwithstanding Clause

Notwithstanding the impact of the language used, I am sure that the general unpopularity of the Conservative party, and particularly that of former Prime Minister Mulroney were important factors in the outcome of the election.

If political parties want to improve their chances of successfully communicating their message to the voting public, they might consider adapting some of the LAB Profile questions for their pre-campaign polls. These questions can also be used to judge the mood of the media, important potential allies in any campaign. The power of the LAB Profile lies in its ability to *measure the mood* of the public and *indicate the language* to which people will be the *most receptive.*

Education and Learning

It is not my intention to criticize public school education in this section, but rather to provide some food for thought.

Why are educational programs designed the way they are? It is usually because the authors believe they have discovered the *best way* to learn a subject. Often they are right about large percentages of the groups they hope to reach, but what about the smaller percentage of students, for whom this is not true?

My comments are about these *other* students, for whom a given model does not work, and who therefore are more likely to drop out of school. In the work I have done with educators on the topic of reducing the number of drop-outs in secondary school, we discussed strategies for keeping kids interested *throughout the school cycle*.

My advice to individual teachers in primary or secondary school, would be to first identify the pupils who are not turned on by class activities. Secondly, profile them to discover what will trigger and maintain their motivation. Once the individual's motivation patterns are known, you can then adapt activities to suit their needs, using the resources and methods available, and inventing some when necessary. Lastly, you will notice a marked improvement in the participation and performance of these previously hard to reach students.

For example, Options students may have difficulty following the prescribed procedure, and as a result, may become frustrated or disruptive in the classroom. These students are more likely to stay motivated and focused if they are given more choice and the possibility to develop their own process. Procedures students may have difficulty knowing how to start an open task. They would appreciate having a procedure to follow to get started. In each case you would need to make sure to use the Influencing Language that matches the student's pattern. "Think of all the possible ways to do this!" (Options) "Here are the first steps to get started." (Procedures)

You can also design or use activities to encourage flexibility in the LAB categories. Following and completing procedures as well as developing options.

For Internal students to stay motivated, they will need to make their own decisions. You can get them to evaluate their own work. When making suggestions to this group, you might want to use phrases such as: "You

177

might want to consider," or "Can I make a suggestion for you to think about?" External students will need lots of feedback to know how well they are doing. To encourage the development of both Internal and External patterns you can provide a balance in activities. Self-evaluation (Internal) and adapting to feedback received (External). You will be able to see and hear who responds best to which patterns merely by observing the students' reactions to the tasks.

Much of someone's ability to use what they have learned is dependent on the *level of confidence* they have about having mastered it. This implies that when someone's Convincer patterns have been satisfied, they are more likely to use the material or do the activity more confidently.

If a child needs 6 or 7 repetitions of a skill to be convinced he knows it, it is unlikely that he will get enough repetition in the course of a school day. My suggestion to teachers, when they notice a child feels unsure of what they have learned, is to ask the Convincer Channel and Mode questions. "How do you know when someone else is good at addition?" "How many times do you have to see them do it right (or hear that they got the right answer, or do the work with them, etc.) for you to be *convinced* that they are good at addition? Then you can assign homework based on the number of repetitions or period of time needed. If the student has a Consistent Convincer Mode, (never completely convinced), you will find that she *knows* she can do it one day and perhaps be unsure the next. Remind her of the previous times when she knew she could do it. She is still the *same* person.

Adult Learners

Learning is a Context in and of itself. The act of learning something is about taking in new material and acquiring it for oneself, while *using* what one has learned requires a different set of behaviours.

As you can probably deduce, this process is a sequence of Contexts: Learn something new in External. Evaluate it in Internal. Use it and determine the results in Internal and External.

For someone to learn something *new*, she will need to be in an External mode. If someone is attempting to take in something new while remaining in Internal mode, the new material will find itself banging up against previously held standards and Criteria within the person. As a result, the ability to actually acquire the new material is limited. In many adult education courses, the learners are asked to put aside, for a while, what they already know about a topic, to facilitate taking in a new way of thinking about it. They are invited to reinstate their critical thinking caps once they have mastered the material.

You will therefore need to help your students shift into an External mode for the *learning* part of the activities. To do this, you will need to establish your credibility, so that they become External *to you*. This is particularly important for adult learners, as any corporate trainer will tell you.

In educational Contexts the LAB Profile is useful in two ways. It can be used to diagnose and plan for students who are not doing well with the programs in vogue. Secondly, it can help teachers understand what patterns they are *unconsciously* encouraging or discouraging as a matter of course.

What Else?

Words That Change Minds is the fruit of my experience using and playing with the LAB Profile in many different Contexts. It can help you just do things as well as to stop and think about them. You will achieve many of your goals while preventing and solving communication problems.

As you use these tools, you will notice what a difference it makes for the others you live and work with. The possibilities are endless for communicating the right way. You can make a big difference, improve what is already good and keep the things that are important to you.

Whether you use this book in great detail or just focus on the big picture, you will understand what is said to you and notice behaviours in new ways. This material can raise many passions and provide for rational thought. When you are alone, working with others around, or together in group harmony, you can feel great about what you accomplish.

If I were you, I would take these tools for myself, use them to guide me and to help me understand how others are different. You will see, hear, and feel the improvements that working with the LAB Profile will instantly provide, over and over again, consistently, for as long as you want.

While I have discussed quite a few applications and ideas, I am sure that there are *many other ways* to use this tool. So I put the question to you:

"Now that you know how to understand and influence people by finding out what will trigger and maintain their motivation, what else would you like to do with it?"

I look forward to hearing from you.

Shelle Rose Charvet
success strategies
220 Townsend Avenue
Burlington, Ontario
Canada L7T 1Z4
phone / fax 1 (905) 639-6468
Email: shelle@wchat.on.ca
CompuServe ID 70274,1035

Appendices

Summaries and Useful Bits

In this section you will find:

- LAB Profile pattern summaries and distribution figures which you can include in reports you give people
- An Influencing Language summary to help you plan what to say or write
- LAB Profile Worksheets to use when profiling people

I hope you have as much fun as I have using

Words That Change Minds.

LAB Profile Pattern Summary

Motivation Traits

How a person triggers their interest and, conversely, what will demotivate them. Each pattern is described below in its extreme form.

LEVEL: Does the person take the initiative or wait for others?

Proactive: Acts with little or no consideration. Motivated by doing.

Reactive: Motivated to wait, analyze, consider and react.

CRITERIA: These words are a person's labels for goodness, rightness and appropriateness in a given context. They incite a positive physical and emotional reaction.

DIRECTION: Is a person's motivational energy centred on goals or problems to be dealt with or avoided?

Toward: These people are motivated to achieve or attain goals. They have trouble recognizing problems. They are good at managing priorities.

Away From: They focus on what may be and is going wrong. They are motivated to solve problems and have trouble keeping focused on goals.

SOURCE: Does the person stay motivated by judgements from external sources or by using their own internal standards?

Internal: They decide based on their own internal standards.

External: They need outside feedback to know how well they are doing.

REASON: Does the person continually look for alternatives or prefer to follow established procedures?

Options: They are compelled to develop and create procedures and systems. Have difficulty following set procedures.

Procedures: They prefer to follow set ways. They get stumped when they have no procedure to follow.

DECISION FACTORS: How does a person react to change and what frequency of change do they need?

Sameness: They want their world to stay the same. They will provoke change only every 15 to 25 years.

Sameness with Exception: They prefer situations to evolve slowly over time. They want major change every 5 to 7 years.

Difference: They want change to be constant and drastic. Major change every 1 to 2 years.

Difference and sameness with exception: They like evolution and revolution. Major change averages every 3 years.

Working Traits

How people treat information, the type of tasks, the environment they need to be most productive and how they go about making decisions.

SCOPE: How large a picture is the person able to work with?

Specific: Details and sequences. They cannot see the overview.

General: Overview, big picture. Can handle details for short periods.

ATTENTION DIRECTION: Does the person pay attention to the nonverbal behaviour of others or attend to their own internal experience?

Self: Attends to own experience. Doesn't notice others' behaviour or voice tone.

Other: Has automatic reflex responses to nonverbal behaviour.

STRESS RESPONSE: How does a person react to the normal stresses of the work environment?

Feeling: Emotional responses to normal levels of stress. Stays in feelings. Not suited for high-stress work.

Choice: Can move in and out of feelings voluntarily. Good at empathy.

Thinking: Do not go into feelings at normal levels of stress. Poor at establishing rapport or showing empathy.

STYLE: What kind of human environment allows the person to work best?

Independent: Alone with sole responsibility.

Proximity: In control of own territory with others around.

Co-operative: Together with others in a team, sharing responsibility.

ORGANIZATION: Does the person concentrate more on thoughts and feelings or on tasks, ideas, systems or tools?

Person: Centered on feelings and thoughts. They become the *task*.

Thing: Centered on tasks, systems, ideas, tools. Getting the job done is the most important thing.

RULE STRUCTURE: Does a person have rules for themselves and others?

My/My: My rules for me. My rules for you. Able to tell others what they expect.

My/.:   My rules for me. I don't care about you.

No/My: Don't know rules for me. My rules for you. Typical middle management pattern.

My/Your: My rules for me. Your rules for you. Hesitant to tell others what to do.

CONVINCER CHANNEL: What type of information does a person need to start the process of getting convinced about something?

See: See evidence.

Hear: Oral presentation or hear something.

Read: Read a report.

Do: Do something.

CONVINCER MODE: What has to happen to the information or evidence previously gathered to make a person become "convinced" of something?

Number of examples: They need to have the data a certain number of times to be convinced.

Automatic: They take a small amount of information and get convinced immediately based on what they extrapolate. They hardly ever change their minds.

Consistent: They are never completely convinced. Every day is a new day and they need to get reconvinced.

Period of time: They need to gather information for a certain duration before their conviction is triggered.

PATTERN DISTRIBUTION

From Rodger Bailey's research, in the context of work, the Language and Behaviour Patterns have the following distribution:

LEVEL

Proactive	Equally Proactive/Reactive	Reactive
15%–20%	60%–65%	15%–20%

DIRECTION

Toward	Equally Toward Away From	Away From
40%	20%	40%

SOURCE

Internal	Equally Internal/External	External
40%	20%	40%

REASON

Options	Equally Options Procedures	Procedures
40%	20%	40%

DECISION FACTORS

Sameness	Sameness with Exception	Difference	Sameness with Exception & Difference
5%	65%	20%	10%

SCOPE

Specific	Equally Specific/General	General
15%	25%	60%

ATTENTION

Self	Other
7%	93%

STRESS RESPONSE

Feeling	Choice	Thinking
15%	70%	15%

STYLE

Independent	Proximity	Co-operative
20%	60%	20%

ORGANIZATION

Person	Equally Person Thing	Thing
15%	30%	55%

RULE STRUCTURE

My/My	My/.	No/My	My/Your
75%	3%	7%	15%

CONVINCER CHANNEL

See	Hear	Read	Do
55%	30%	3%	12%

CONVINCER MODE

Number of Examples	Automatic	Consistent	Period of Time
52%	8%	15%	25%

Influencing Language Summary

Motivation Traits

LEVEL
Proactive: do it; go for it; jump in; now; get it done; don't wait
Reactive: understand; think about; wait; analyze; consider; might; could; would; the important thing is to . . .

DIRECTION
Toward: attain; obtain; have; get; include; achieve
Away From: avoid; steer clear of; not have; get rid of; exclude; away from

SOURCE
External: so and so thinks; the impact will be; the feedback you'll get; the approval you'll get; others will notice; give references; results
Internal: only you can decide; you know its up to you; what do you think; you might want to consider

REASON
Options: break the rules just for them; opportunity; choice; expanding; options; alternatives; possibilities
Procedures: speak in procedures: first; then; after which; the right way; tried and true; tell them about the procedures they will get to use

DECISION FACTORS
Sameness: same as; in common; as you always do; like before; unchanged; as you know
Sameness with Exception:
        more; better; less; same except; evolving; progress; gradual improvement
Difference: new; totally different; completely changed; switch; shift; unique; revolutionary; brand new; one of a kind
Sameness with Exception and Difference:
        (both sameness with exception and difference vocabulary will work)

Working Traits

SCOPE
Specific: exactly; precisely; specifically (and give lots of details in sequence)

General: the big picture; essentially; the important thing is; in general; concepts

ATTENTION DIRECTION
Self: (keep communication focused on the content)

Other: (influenced by the depth of rapport)

STRESS RESPONSE
Feeling: happy; intense; exciting; mind boggling; wonderful

Choice: empathy; appropriate; makes good sense and feels right

Thinking: clear thinking; logical; rational; cold reality; hard facts; statistics

STYLE
Independent: do it alone; by yourself; you alone; without interruption; total responsibility and control

Proximity: you'll be in charge with others involved; you'll direct; lead; your responsibility is X; their's is Y

Co-operative: us; we; together, all of us; team; group; share responsibility; do it together; let's

ORGANIZATION
Person: (use personal pronouns and people's names); feelings; thoughts; feel good; people

Thing: (impersonal pronouns) things; systems; process; task; job; goal; organization; company; accomplishments

RULE STRUCTURE
no particular words or phrases—you can match these patterns as you talk

CONVINCER CHANNEL
See: (must see data to get convinced)

Hear: (must hear data to get convinced)

Read: (must read data to get convinced)

Do: (must do it, or work with someone to get convinced)

CONVINCER MODE
Number of Examples:
         (use their number)
Automatic: assume; benefit of the doubt
Consistent: try it; each time you use it; daily; every time; consistent
Period of Time: (match period of time)

Motivation Traits

	Level	
(no question for Level)	_____	Proactive
	_____	Reactive
	Critiera	

	Direction	
• What do you want in a *(job)?*	_____	Toward
	_____	Away From
• Why is that *(criteria)* important?	**Source**	
(ask up to 3 times)	_____	Internal
	_____	External
• How do you know you have done a good job *(at . . . .)?*	**Reason**	
	_____	Options
	_____	Procedures
• Why did you choose *(your current job)?*	**Decision Factors**	
	_____	Sameness
• What is the relationship between *(your work this year and last year)?*	_____	Sameness with Exception
	_____	Difference
	_____	Sameness with Exception & Difference

Working Traits

	Scope	
(no questions for Scope and Attention Direction)	_____	Specific
	_____	General
	Attention Direction	
	_____	Self
	_____	Other
• Tell me about a *(work situation)* that gave you trouble.	**Stress Response**	
	_____	Feelings
	_____	Choice
	_____	Thinking
• Tell me about a *(work situation)* that was *(criteria)*. *(wait for answer)*	**Style**	
• What did you like about it?	_____	Independent
	_____	Proximity
	_____	Co-operation
	Organization	
	_____	Person
	_____	Thing
• What is a good way for you to increase the chances for your success at *(your work . . .)?*	**Rule Structure**	
	_____	My/My
• What is a good way for someone else to increase the chances for their success at *(their work . . .)?*	_____	My/.(period)
	_____	No/My
	_____	My/Your

• How do you know that someone else *(as equal of yours)* is good at their *(work . . .)?*	**Convincer**			
• How many times do you have to *(see, hear, read, do)* that to be convinced that they are good?	_____	See	_____	Nb of Examples
	_____	Hear	_____	Automatic
	_____	Read	_____	Consistent
	_____	Do	_____	Period of Time

Motivation Traits

(no question for Level)

Level
_____ Proactive
_____ Reactive

Critiera

- What do you want in a *(job)?*

  _____

- Why is that *(criteria)* important?
  (ask up to 3 times)

  _____

- How do you know you have done a good job
  (at . . . . .)?

  _____

- Why did you choose *(your current job)?*

  _____

- What is the relationship between *(your work this year and last year)?*

Direction
_____ Toward
_____ Away From

Source
_____ Internal
_____ External

Reason
_____ Options
_____ Procedures

Decision Factors
_____ Sameness
_____ Sameness with Exception
_____ Difference
_____ Sameness with Exception & Difference

Working Traits

(no questions for Scope and Attention Direction)

Scope
_____ Specific
_____ General

Attention Direction
_____ Self
_____ Other

- Tell me about a *(work situation)* that gave you trouble.

  _____

- Tell me about a *(work situation)* that was *(criteria)*.
  (wait for answer)
- What did you like about it?

  _____

Stress Response
_____ Feelings
_____ Choice
_____ Thinking

Style
_____ Independent
_____ Proximity
_____ Co-operation

Organization
_____ Person
_____ Thing

- What is a good way for you to increase the chances for your success at *(your work . . .)?*
- What is a good way for someone else to increase the chances for their success at *(their work . . .)?*
- How do you know that someone else *(as equal of yours)* is good at their *(work . . .)?*
- How many times do you have to *(see, hear, read, do)* that to be convinced that they are good?

Rule Structure
_____ My/My
_____ My/.(period)
_____ No/My
_____ My/Your

Convincer
_____ See   _____ Nb of Examples
_____ Hear   _____ Automatic
_____ Read   _____ Consistent
_____ Do   _____ Period of Time

Resources

Rose Charvet, Shelle; **Understanding and Triggering Motivation.** The LAB Profile audio cassette series, available in English or French from Success Strategies, 220 Townsend Avenue, Burlington, Ontario, Canada L7T 1Z4 phone/fax 1 (905)639–6468 Email: shelle@wchat.on.ca CompuServe ID 70274,1035

Bailey, Rodger; **Hiring, Managing and Selling for Peak Performance.** LAB Profile Self-study kit with audio tapes and manual, available from Georgian Bay NLP Centre, 52 Sykes Street N., Meaford, Ontario, Canada N4L 1R2 phone 1 (519) 538–1194.

They have a full catalogue of NLP and related books and tapes.

For LAB TRAINING AND CONSULTING

Shelle Rose Charvet, Success Strategies / Stratégies de réussite,

220 Townsend Avenue, Burlington, Ontario, Canada L7T 1Z4 phone/fax 1(905)639–6468

Index